GERARD RICHARDSON

Mind–Bending True Stories

Fascinating Facts, Bizarre Tales and Trivia from History, Science, and Culture

Contents

Introduction

History is more than just important dates and great conquests; it's also made up of moments so bizarre, they barely seem real. Dive into the odd corners of the past, where truth is stranger, and often more entertaining than fiction. From animals that became war heroes to scientific experiments that sound like they were dreamt up in a mad scientist's lab, these stories remind us that human history is wonderfully weird.

Among these strange tales, Mike the Headless Chicken, who lived for 18 months after his head was chopped off in 1945. He became a sideshow sensation, touring the country and proving that sometimes, life finds a way, no matter how bizarre the circumstances.

Consider Wojtek, a Syrian brown bear adopted by Polish soldiers during World War II. Wojtek helped carry ammunition during the Battle of Monte Cassino, walking on his hind legs to pass shells to his fellow soldiers. After the war, he retired to the Edinburgh Zoo, beloved by all who knew his remarkable story.

Not all tales are whimsical. Take Project A119, a top-secret U.S. plan during the Cold War to detonate a nuclear bomb on the Moon. Why? To one-up the Soviet Union in the space race, potentially altering the moon's appearance with a mushroom cloud visible from Earth. Fortunately, this plan was never executed, leaving the moon as the serene presence we know today.

These stories, from a chicken that refused to die to a bear in combat and a nuclear moon, are mere glimpses into the strange sagas that history has to offer. As we turn the pages, prepare to delve deeper into each bizarre incident, exploring what these anomalies tell us about human creativity, resilience, and the extraordinary lengths to which people—and animals—can go.

Each chapter promises a journey into the less-traveled paths of the past, uncovering events that defy belief and challenge our understanding of what is truly possible. Welcome to a world where the peculiar and the profound blend seamlessly, crafting a history that entertains as much as it enlightens.

Napoleon's Bunny Attack

In the summer of 1807, Napoleon Bonaparte likely felt invincible, with everything seemingly going his way. Yet, during this period, a curious and unusual incident unfolded, which we will delve into in this episode. We'll explore the various accounts of what transpired that day with Napoleon, though these stories vary in detail, they generally agree on a core sequence of events.

To set the scene, in June 1807, Napoleon clinched a significant victory at the Battle of Friedland. This triumph compelled Russian Emperor Alexander I to agree to a truce, culminating in the Treaty of Tilsit. For Napoleon, this treaty not only marked a career pinnacle but also confirmed his supremacy in mainland Europe. In a celebratory mood, he planned a rabbit hunt, which was organized by his Chief of Staff, Alexander Berthier. Berthier, eager to impress, spared no expense in the preparations. Although reports vary, some suggest he gathered as many as 3,000 rabbits for the event—an undoubtedly lavish figure.

On the day of the hunt, the plan was to release the rabbits into a field. However, the execution was far from smooth. Upon release, instead of scattering, the rabbits charged towards Napoleon and his party. Initially, the scene was met with laughter; however, the humor quickly faded as the rabbits persisted in their advance. The hunters, armed with bullwhips, hunting crops, and sticks, tried in vain to repel the mass of rabbits, but to no avail. Eventually, the overwhelmed party retreated, with Napoleon having to push his way through the rabbits to escape in his carriage.

The hunt was a fiasco, and blame fell on Berthier. The primary oversight was his choice of domesticated rather than wild rabbits. These animals, accustomed to human contact, associated people with feeding rather than fear. Furthermore, it's speculated that the rabbits were not fed during transport, intensifying their hunger when released.

What can we glean from this peculiar story? It seems the rabbits, behaving less like wild animals and more like expectant pets, disrupted the hunt entirely, resulting in no sport and only chaos. This event, likely embellished over time, serves as a humorous footnote in history, illustrating a moment when even Napoleon was outmaneuvered, not by armies, but by rabbits. In the end, if there's any truth to the tale, the responsibility lies with Berthier, and it seems that on that day, the rabbits unwittingly claimed victory.

Death of Henry I

In November 1135, Henry I, the first King of England and son of William the Conqueror, was around 66 or 67 years old, though his exact birthdate is uncertain. He had been reigning for 35 years. At the time, he was not in London but in Normandy, staying at his lodge in Leon La Foret for a hunting trip. On November 25, he suddenly became gravely ill. A popular tale suggests his sickness was due to consuming a surfeit of lampreys, a type of fish, but historical documents suggest this detail might be exaggerated. According to William of Malmesbury, a contemporary monk and chronicler, Henry fell ill suddenly while hunting in Lyon and his condition worsened over the following days. Orderic Vitalis, another chronicler, notes that Henry planned another hunting trip the day before he fell ill during the night, without mentioning a specific cause for his illness.

William of Newburgh, born around the time of Henry's death and not a contemporary, simply stated that upon completing his life and reign, Henry "slept with his fathers." He likely had access to adults from 1135 and to now-lost documents. The connection of Henry's death to lampreys is specifically mentioned only by Henry of Huntington, an archdeacon alive during Henry's lifetime and well-placed to gather information from influential contemporaries. Although it is unclear when Huntington wrote about the monarch's death, it was certainly before his own death in 1157, possibly closer to the actual event.

One reason to approach his chronicle with caution is its moralizing tone and his tendency to invent details to enhance the narrative, such as fabricated speeches he attributed to historical figures at pivotal moments. With this in mind, here is his account of the King's death: After returning from hunting at Sandini in the Wood of Lions, the King ate some lampreys, a dish he was fond of, despite their adverse effects on him and against his physician's advice to abstain. The narrative mentions that, driven by human nature's tendency to seek forbidden things, the King ignored this wise counsel, leading to ill humors and severe symptoms that precipitated a sudden and extreme disturbance. His aged body could not withstand the strain, and nature's struggle to expel the burden resulted in an acute fever. Eventually, his resistance failed, and he died on the first day of December.

From this account, it appears that the King was advised against eating lampreys entirely due to their disagreeable effects, but he indulged nonetheless and soon fell ill, exhibiting symptoms like fever. There was no mention of an excessive quantity, implying he might not have consumed more than usual. Interestingly, his inability to tolerate the fish, despite his preference for them, suggests a possible health issue such as an allergy or a condition like an ulcer, rather than mere indulgence. It seems unlikely to be an allergy, as that would have been a persistent issue, and it is doubtful he would have continued consuming lampreys had they consistently caused illness. Thus, an issue like an ulcer, emerging in his later years, seems more plausible, with the King unwilling to forsake a delicacy he had always enjoyed.

There is also the possibility that Henry's diet was unrelated to his demise; perhaps he caught a chill while hunting, given it was November. Moreover, the entire lamprey story might have been a fabrication by Huntington, who liked to impart a moral lesson in his writings, as seen in his portrayal of the King's defiance as a classic case of humans seeking forbidden pleasures. Alternatively, Huntington might have been better informed about the King's final days, which is why he provides details others do not.

Regarding the preparation of bodies for burial in medieval times, some accounts are more detailed than others. The Anglo-Saxon Chronicle briefly states that King Henry's sons and friends transported his body to England for burial at Reading. Orderic Vitalis, elaborating on the burial site, mentioned that Henry had requested to be interred there due to his founding of a monastery for 200 monks. Vitalis also detailed the respectful escort of the King's body to the seaside, involving great lords urged by the Archbishop and Owen, Bishop of Evreux, to honor their master's remains.

Vitalis provided a clinical description of the embalming process: the body, described as very fat, was opened by a skilled surgeon and treated with sweet spices. The entrails were placed in an urn and deposited in the church of Saint Mary Dupre, which his mother had initiated and he had completed. The King's knights and household staff accompanied the body to Caen, where it remained for nearly four weeks, awaiting favorable winds. After Christmas, monks transported the body across the sea to England, where it received a dignified burial in the Abbey Church at Reading, overseen by his successor, King Stephen, bishops, and nobles.

Robert de Monte's account aligns with Vitalis', detailing the body's reception in Rouen with great ceremony, the burial of the heart, tongue, and bowels at the monastery de Prey altar, and the preservation of the body in salt and hides until it could be transported to England. Within 12 days of Christmas, the body was interred at the Saint Mary of Reading monastery, which Henry had founded and endowed, in a ceremony attended by King Stephen, Archbishop William of Canterbury, and many nobles.

William of Malmesbury noted that his information on Henry's death came from the Archbishop of Rion, a highly credible source. He provided the initial indications that the body was in poor condition, writing that the body, escorted royally and carried in turns by the nobility, was brought to Ryong. There, in a secluded area of the main church, it was disemboweled to prevent putrefaction, which could distress those nearby. The intestines were buried at the Monastery of Saint Mary Dupree near the city, a site Henry had notably honored, initiated by his mother. The body remained in Khan until the tempestuous weather calmed, a detail corroborated by other sources regarding the adverse weather conditions.

William of Newburgh, though not a contemporary as he was born around the time of Henry's death, also discussed the body's rapid deterioration. According to him, after the removal of the brain and intestines and subsequent embalming, the body was sewn into skins and transported from Normandy to England for burial at Reading, a monastery Henry had significantly supported. Notably, the man employed to remove the brain succumbed to an infection from the unbearable stench, ironically giving the deceased king the ability to cause death, akin to the Biblical figure Elisha reanimating the dead.

Henry of Huntington, a contemporary with access to reliable information, corroborated this account, suggesting that he could have been Newburgh's source. Unlike others who were more circumspect in describing the state of the corpse, Huntington provided a stark depiction. He detailed that Henry's body was taken to Ruin, where parts including his brain and eyes were deposited. The body, treated with multiple cuts and heavily salted, was encased in ox hides to contain the foul odors, which were so potent they were considered pestilential. The man tasked with severing the head and removing the brain, despite taking precautions with a linen veil, also died from the exposure, his compensation proving costly in the end.

Despite extensive measures like using salt and ox hides, fluids continued to leak from the body, collected in vessels under the bier, causing distress and fainting among those handling the remains. This vivid account concludes with a reflection on the transience of earthly glory, contrasting the king's once dazzling appearance, adorned with jewels and gold, with the grotesque decay of his corpse.

Ultimately, Henry's remains were transported to England and laid to rest within twelve days of Christmas at the Abbey of Reading, which he had founded and endowed richly, marking a somber end to his storied reign.

Dancing Plague of 1518

On July 14, 1518, just a week before the festival of Mary Magdalene, Frau Trophia emerged from her half-timbered house into the sweltering heat of summer and began to dance. Her movements were not the joyful jigs typically set to music but rather awkward, jerky motions, hopping painfully from one foot to the other. Despite her husband's pleas to stop and come inside, she continued dancing into the evening. As the sun set over Strausburg, a crowd of puzzled onlookers gathered, witnessing Frau Trophia's inability to cease her frantic dancing. Hours later, drenched in sweat and still twitching, she collapsed into a brief, necessary sleep.

With dawn, Frau Trophia resumed her odd dance and persisted for another two days, despite increasing exhaustion and injuries. Her feet became bruised and bloody, her actions increasingly erratic and violent as fatigue overwhelmed her. The spectacle drew crowds from all social strata, from ragged beggars to opulent nobles, all speculating about the cause of her condition. Initial rumors suggested she was feigning the dance to annoy her dance-loathing husband.

The Swiss physician and chronicler Paracelsus theorized it was a form of disobedience toward her husband, linking her actions to a refusal of a prior request. As her condition worsened, suspicions of possession or divine punishment arose, reflecting 16th-century beliefs about women's susceptibility to witchcraft due to their supposed lustful nature and weaker morals.

After four grueling days, with her shoes soaked in blood and her expression one of agonizing pain, it was concluded that she was being punished by a vengeful saint. Frau Trophia was hastily taken to the shrine of Saint Vitus in the Vosges Mountains. Her ordeal was henceforth known as Saint Vitus's Dance, recorded by community members including officials, preachers, and merchants, marking a bizarre chapter in their local history.

Within days, the streets of Strasbourg were filled with people overtaken by a relentless urge to dance. This rapidly evolving craze affected everyone from all walks of life—some in leather shoes, others in clogs, and many barefoot. They danced with frenzied intensity, their limbs flailing as exhaustion ravaged their bodies. The toll of the dance became deadly, and although the exact number of fatalities is unclear, reports indicate up to 15 individuals per day succumbed, dehydrated and starved amidst the July heat. By late August, the epidemic finally subsided, leaving the community frightened and bewildered, mourning those lost.

This phenomenon was not unprecedented. In 1017, in the German village of Kolbeek, several people reportedly danced uncontrollably in a graveyard. According to legend, a priest, outraged by their behavior, cursed them to dance for an entire year. Whether this event truly occurred or serves as a cautionary tale against the medieval condemnation of revelry remains uncertain.

Another historical account by Gerald of Wales in 1188 describes an annual religious ceremony in Saint Alderman's Church in South Wales. There, people gathered in the churchyard, singing and dancing until collapsing. They then mimed laborious tasks they had skipped during the week—sewing, weaving, or shoe repair—as if in a trance, a scene eerily reminiscent of criticisms of my one-man cabaret show.

These instances suggest a pattern of dancing manias, including the tragic event in 1247 Erfurt, where about 100 children danced out of town to a neighboring village, only to collapse in exhaustion. Many never recovered, suffering lifelong convulsions and fatigue. This episode likely inspired the grim legend of the Pied Piper of Hamelin, located over 150 miles from Erfurt. In the tale, the Piper, unpaid for clearing the town of rats, exacts his revenge by enchanting the town's children with his pipe, leading them into a cave, never to be seen again.

Shortly after the peculiar event in Erfurt in 1278, citizens of Maastricht, now in the Netherlands, danced onto a bridge over the river Moselle. Tragically, the medieval bridge collapsed under the strain, killing everyone involved. The Church viewed this as divine retribution for the dancers' irreverence. A more widespread outbreak swept through the Rhineland in the summer of 1374, affecting areas from Gentination in the north to Mars and Strasbourg in the south. Thousands, seized by a compulsive need to dance and scream in agony, called out to God and His saints for relief. Witnesses described the dancers as shouting like lunatics that they would die without tight sheets wrapped around their waists, hinting at demonic possession. Many ended up at a deserted chapel near Trier, where they camped before resuming their frantic dancing.

The question arises: How did the uncontrollable dancing of one woman evolve into a full-blown epidemic? Was this self-inflicted pain a form of penance, much like the self-flagellation practiced during the Black Death? Flagellants believed true repentance required physical pain and public humiliation. Physicians at the time, however, attributed the dancing to a physical ailment caused by an overheating of the blood due to an imbalance of the humors, dismissing supernatural or astrological explanations. Their proposed remedy? Ironically, more dancing, under the assumption that intense sweating could purge the overheated blood, despite the risks of heart attacks and strokes from exhaustion and the sun.

Prior to the dancing epidemic, the region faced famine, rising superstitions, and soaring grain prices, leading to widespread hunger. Following this, Strasbourg was hit by smallpox in the spring, plague in early summer, and a mysterious sweating sickness later in the year. By early 1518, many had perished from the cold and starvation. The surviving populace sought divine intervention through increased prayers and masses, hoping to placate an apparently wrathful God.

Such extreme stress levels could have sparked a mass psychogenic illness, a phenomenon where physical symptoms of an illness manifest among groups under stress without an actual contagion. Notable examples include the Salem witch trials, driven by religious extremism and isolation, and the 1962 laughter epidemic in Tanganyika, among overworked students. Given the religious and existential fears prevalent at the time, conditions were ripe for such an outbreak in Strasbourg. This hypothesis of mass hysteria, combined with historical accounts of ergot poisoning—a fungus causing hallucinations and convulsions known as Saint Anthony's fire—offers some explanation, though it fails to account for the rhythmic dancing reported.

Overall, the evidence suggests that the medieval dancing plagues were likely mass psychoses, fueled by years of hardship, religious zeal, and societal anxiety. The 1518 event marked the last such outbreak in Europe, making it one of the most bizarre episodes in medieval history.

The Voynich Manuscript

The Voynich Manuscript, a peculiar 15th-century text, stands out due to its collection of bizarre illustrations, from unidentifiable flora to cryptic celestial charts and enigmatic figures engaging with unknown machinery. Within its pages lies an enigmatic script crafted in an unknown language, adorned with a unique alphabet and grammar, which remains undeciphered to this day, despite claims by some to have cracked its codes. This manuscript is one of the most debated books in history, surrounded by endless theories about its origins, meaning, and purpose. Let's delve into the mysteries of the Voynich Manuscript.

Officially cataloged as Beinecke MS-408 but popularly known as the Voynich Manuscript, it bears the name of Wilfred Voynich, an antique collector who acquired it in 1912. Following his passing, it was bequeathed to Yale University's Beinecke Rare Book and Manuscript Library, where it is preserved and occasionally displayed to the public, though a digital version is also available online. Despite its modest size and worn condition, the manuscript's interior reveals a world of peculiar illustrations and text that defies interpretation. The text is particularly enigmatic, penned in an unidentifiable language that has baffled cryptographers for centuries.

Believed to be of medieval European origin, the manuscript's imagery and style are distinctively characteristic of that era. Uncovering the manuscript's secrets involves exploring its provenance, authorship, and authenticity. The tale begins with Wilfred Voynich, a London-based rare book dealer. Voynich acquired the manuscript under mysterious circumstances in 1912 from the Jesuit College in Rome, which was facing financial difficulties and had planned to sell its collection to the Vatican. The circumstances of how Voynich came into possession of the manuscript remain unclear, with some suggesting he may have acquired it illicitly.

The manuscript captivated Voynich and attracted the attention of eminent scholars, including William Friedman, a renowned cryptologist who spent decades attempting to decipher it. Despite extensive efforts, the manuscript's code remained unsolved. After Voynich's death, the manuscript eventually made its way to Yale in 1969. Some speculate that Voynich might have forged the manuscript, a theory fueled by his evasiveness about its origins. However, carbon dating conducted in 2009 confirmed the manuscript's creation between 1404 and 1438, with materials and techniques consistent with that period, countering claims of forgery.

Further legitimacy comes from a 1665 letter discovered with the manuscript, written by scientist Johannes Marci to Athanasius Kircher, mentioning its previous ownership by Emperor Rudolf II who believed Roger Bacon, a 13th-century English philosopher known for his comprehensive works on science and alchemy, was the author. Despite such historical connections, the true author remains unknown, contributing to the enduring enigma of the Voynich Manuscript.

While in Prague, the Voynich Manuscript changed hands several times. One notable owner, George Baresch, described the book as containing "writing in unknown characters with pictures of herbs and varied images of stars and other things." Another owner, Jacobi a Tepenec, left his signature so faint inside the cover that only multi-spectral imaging can reveal it. Tepenec, a courtier in Prague and the head of Emperor Rudolph's botanical gardens, likely had an interest in the manuscript's extensive plant illustrations.

After its time in Prague, the manuscript disappeared for 250 years before resurfacing at the Jesuit College. It is speculated that Athanasius Kircher, the recipient of the initial letter about the manuscript and a Jesuit himself, may have transported it from Prague to Rome. In 1912, Wilfred Voynich acquired the manuscript under mysterious circumstances, adding another chapter to its colorful history of ownership. Radiocarbon dating pins the creation of the book to the early 15th century. It remains anonymous, as Roger Bacon, once speculated to be the author, had died a century earlier.

The manuscript then remains undocumented until it appears again in Prague, handled by various individuals including Emperor Rudolf II. After being stored likely in a Jesuit library in Rome, it ultimately fell into the hands of Wilfred Voynich. The intriguing history of the Voynich Manuscript is just one aspect of this extraordinary document, urging us to examine its contents more closely.

In the absence of decipherable text, the illustrations provide the best insights into the manuscript's meaning and purpose. The book is divided into sections, each focusing on a different topic. The largest section, about half of the manuscript, is filled with plant sketches. Each page features a single illustration accompanied by what seems to be a description. These plants range from bizarre to alien-looking, with some resembling real-life plants, while others remain unidentifiable.

In the medieval era, such herbals were common, serving as early natural encyclopedias that cataloged plant life, their appearances, where they grew, and their medicinal uses. However, the Voynich Manuscript stands out for its unusual illustrations, which are crudely colored and roughly drawn, suggesting they might have been sketched based on second-hand descriptions, a common practice in the medieval period.

Following the botanical section are two sections dedicated to the stars, filled with beautiful circular charts, some of which unfold into larger spreads. These sections feature recognizable zodiac symbols and are heavily annotated, possibly indicating astrological significance, which was often linked with medicine in medieval times.

Sandwiched between the astrological and cosmological sections is one filled with drawings of miniature naked women bathing in elaborate settings, hinting at early forms of hydrotherapy believed to benefit specific body parts. This ties into the health-focused themes seen throughout the manuscript.

The book circles back to plant drawings towards the end but with a different layout, showing roots and herbs alongside mysteriously colored cylinders, possibly containers, adding another layer of mystery to the enigmatic Voynich Manuscript.

The sections of the Voynich Manuscript that feature laboratory-like equipment, similar to those used in alchemy, suggest a possible medical or scientific focus, aligning with the rest of the manuscript's content. Other alchemical texts from the same period also contain illustrations of beakers and test tubes, but those typically involve precious metals and stones rather than plants and herbs. It's plausible that the depicted equipment belonged to an apothecary, who would have created herbal medicines, adding a layer of practical application to the manuscript's mystique.

The final section of the manuscript is the most enigmatic, consisting entirely of text that remains untranslated, with what appear to be star-like bullet points beside capitalized letters. This has led some to label it as 'recipes,' though this could be a misleading designation since the content's true nature remains unknown. With the manuscript concluding this text section, it suggests that the manuscript might function as a health almanac, linking medieval knowledge from herbals to astrological charts, and even bathing rituals.

Focusing on the writing, the manuscript employs a unique alphabet that blends familiar Latin script characters with numeral-like and tall, looping characters nicknamed 'gallows' for their resemblance to a hangman's scaffold. This alphabet features 22 letters, occasionally interspersed with unique symbols, forming words that vary in length and are separated by spaces.

The manuscript is thought to be a cipher, where language is disguised by substituting letters for symbols. This method was used historically to secure sensitive information, as seen in the Copial Cipher, which was eventually decoded and found to contain secret society rituals. Deciphering such a cipher typically involves identifying the underlying language, which provides clues to unlocking the code.

The Voynich Manuscript, however, defies typical linguistic patterns, presenting a challenge with its absence of recognizable language fingerprints. It contains patterns and repetition suggestive of a structured language, not random gibberish, indicating sophisticated encoding possibly involving two different languages, dubbed Language A and Language B. These could represent different sections of the manuscript, possibly authored by different individuals.

Word distribution analysis in the manuscript reveals a natural language pattern where common and rare words fall into a predictable hierarchy, suggesting an underlying linguistic structure. However, the manuscript's predictability in letter patterns and word positions differs significantly from natural languages, indicating a highly formulaic and perhaps artificially constructed language.

Further analysis involves identifying keywords specific to various sections, using the illustrations as context clues. For instance, common words in the plant and root sections might relate to herbal properties. While this doesn't decipher the actual words, it underscores the manuscript's thematic consistency and hints at the presence of a coherent, if elusive, language.

In summary, the Voynich Manuscript remains a profound mystery, blending elements of historical herbal and astrological knowledge with enigmatic text and illustrations. Its decipherment continues to elude experts, presenting a tantalizing puzzle that merges the intrigue of ancient science with the complexity of cryptographic challenges.

Analyzing the distribution of words in the Voynich Manuscript reveals a pattern of common and rare words, suggesting it's not random gibberish but a structured language. The predictability in how the letters are arranged far exceeds that of any known language, and searching for keywords shows clusters of unique words in the plant and root sections, indicating their relevance to these topics. This complexity is why cryptographers have struggled to decipher the manuscript—it appears to be a language, yet it is unlike any familiar language.

Many have claimed to have decoded or translated the Voynich Manuscript. Some theories suggest the mystery language could be a Romance language— descended from Latin like Italian, French, and Spanish—and propose it might be an abbreviated form of Latin, anagrams of Italian, or even a proto-Romance language. The only readable words in the manuscript, the names of months, are in Occitan, a cousin of French, fitting the historical and geographical context. Yet, none of these theories have been conclusively proven. Other suggestions range from Ukrainian to Turkish to English, and some even propose it's written in an Aztec language, considering the depiction of plants possibly native to Mexico.

In 2016, a notable theory suggested it was an encrypted form of Hebrew. Researchers, using an algorithm, translated a sentence but had to rely on Google Translate, resulting in a grammatically nonsensical Hebrew sentence. This approach, while initially creating buzz, was criticized for its reliance on automated translation tools.

The theory that the Voynich Manuscript might represent a long-lost language, like the Rongo Rongo of Easter Island, is tantalizing. However, there's no evidence of a European language isolate that matches the manuscript's content, making this theory as elusive as the language itself.

Many skeptics argue that the manuscript might be a hoax, a medieval prank using a constructed language to create seemingly meaningful but ultimately nonsensical content. The uniform predictability of the letters and the complete absence of corrections or errors in the manuscript, which is unusual for medieval texts, support this idea. Yet, considering the expense and effort involved in creating such a manuscript, dismissing it as a mere joke seems insufficient.

An alternative theory posits that the manuscript could be written in a constructed language, similar to modern examples like Esperanto or the languages created by J.R.R. Tolkien. The manuscript's unique alphabet and the structured yet unfamiliar linguistic patterns could suggest an artificially created language, possibly explaining its undecipherable content.

Many constructed languages originated as early attempts to create a universal language, often spearheaded by philosophers and scientists eager to have their research understood across linguistic boundaries. The Voynich Manuscript may represent one such attempt, particularly given its scientific content. It could have employed an experimental language aimed at broader accessibility, contrasting with a cipher's purpose to conceal information. Ironically, if this was the intention, the language's rules have since been lost, rendering the manuscript unreadable to modern audiences.

While no theory is entirely flawless, and there are challenges to overcome, constructed languages usually draw on one or more natural languages for their structure. For example, Esperanto blends elements from various European languages, and Tolkien's Quenya is inspired by Finnish. If the Voynich Manuscript indeed utilizes a constructed language, it likely would have a natural language as its foundation—possibly even two, given the manuscript's dual linguistic content. Latin, the academic lingua franca of the medieval era, would be a plausible choice.

Yet, the Voynich Manuscript's language remains a puzzle, possibly destined to remain unsolved, continuing to intrigue and challenge scholars and cryptologists alike.

Phineas Gage

On September 13, 1848, Phineas Gage was working on the excavation of rocks for the construction of a railroad track along the Rutland and Burlington Railroad near Cavendish, Vermont. Just before the incident, Gage was preparing for an explosion by packing a borehole with explosive powder using a tamping iron. A spark from the tamping iron ignited the powder, propelling the iron through Gage's skull. It entered below his left cheekbone and exited through the top of his head, landing about 30 yards away, covered in blood and brain tissue.

To understand the severity of the damage caused by the iron, consider its dimensions. The tamping iron was 3 feet 8 inches long (1.11 meters), 1.25 inches (3.18 cm) in diameter at one end, and tapered to 0.25 inches (0.6 cm) at the other, weighing roughly 13 pounds (6 kg). After the rod penetrated his skull, it remains uncertain if Gage lost consciousness, but he was soon walking and talking. Mere minutes after the accident, he was sitting upright in an oxcart on the 3/4 mile journey to his home. There, he was treated by Dr. Edward H. Williams. Upon arrival, Gage greeted him with, "Doctor, here is business enough for you." Dr. Williams noticed the wound and the distinct pulsations of the brain before even stepping out of his carriage. The top of Gage's head resembled an inverted funnel, as if a wedge-shaped object had passed through from the bottom upwards.

While Dr. Williams attended to him, Gage explained how he was injured to those around him, though Dr. Williams initially doubted his account. Gage insisted the bar had passed through his head. During this conversation, Gage vomited, expelling about half a teacup of brain tissue onto the floor.

Dr. John Martyn Harlow later took over his care, documenting Gage's recovery and the notable changes in his personality, providing insights into the role of the frontal cortex in shaping personality. Initial treatment involved cleaning the wound, removing small bone fragments, and repositioning larger, displaced pieces.

The large wound on top of Phineas Gage's head was sealed with adhesive straps and covered with a wet compress to facilitate drainage into the dressings. Days later, his exposed brain became infected, plunging him into a semi-comatose state, from which he miraculously recovered to his family's relief and surprise. Shortly thereafter, Dr. Harlow had to drain 8 fluid ounces of pus from an abscess under Gage's scalp.

Despite these challenges, merely three and a half months post-accident, Gage was leading a relatively normal life. This was in stark contrast to the exaggerated stories that circulated, which have since been largely debunked as myths due to lack of evidence. However, those close to him noticed subtle changes in his personality and behavior.

In 1868, Dr. Harlow reported in the Bulletin of the Massachusetts Medical Society that Gage's contractors, who previously saw him as a highly competent foreman, found his mental changes too significant to reinstate him. His behavior became unpredictable and disrespectful, often using coarse language which was uncharacteristic of him before the injury. He showed little respect for others, resisted advice, and displayed erratic and inconsistent behavior, frequently devising and then abandoning plans.

These alterations led acquaintances to remark that he was "no longer Gage." No longer seen as the reliable foreman by the railroad company, he took up various jobs including a brief stint at a livery stable in New Hampshire. He later worked as a stagecoach driver in Chile for seven years until his health began to fail.

Recent findings from 2008 suggest that prior to his health decline in Chile, Gage had largely regained his social abilities and led a relatively normal life. After his health deteriorated, he moved to San Francisco with his mother. He suffered a series of epileptic seizures and died on May 20, 1860, at the age of 36, nearly 12 years after his accident.

Dr. Harlow, who assumed he would never hear of Gage again, was informed of his death in 1866. At his request, Gage's family exhumed his skull and sent it, along with the tamping iron that had caused the injury, to Dr. Harlow in Massachusetts. Today, both the skull and the iron are exhibited at the Warren Anatomical Museum at Harvard University School of Medicine.

Wojtek the Bear

In 1942, a group of Polish soldiers, recently liberated from prisons and labor camps, discovered an unlikely companion—a brown bear cub. Captivated by its playful nature and friendly demeanor, the soldiers adopted the cub, treating him as a member of their unit. As the cub grew into a bear, and as World War II escalated, Wojtek, as he was later named, stood alongside the soldiers in battle, earning himself an official position in the Polish military.

The conflict had begun on September 1, 1939, with Poland facing invasions from Germany from the north and west, and from Soviet forces from the east on September 17. Following these invasions, over 400,000 Polish prisoners were deported to Siberian labor camps. This situation arose from the German-Soviet non-aggression pact, which later disintegrated in 1941 when Hitler launched an invasion of the Soviet Union. Reacting sharply to the betrayal, Stalin released the Polish prisoners to aid in the fight against Germany.

As these soldiers journeyed from Siberia to Iran, they encountered a young shepherd carrying a Syrian brown bear cub in a sack—his mother had been killed by hunters. The soldiers were charmed by the cub's vivacious spirit and exchanged goods with the shepherd to adopt him. Naming the bear Wojtek, which translates to "joyful soldier," the soldiers embraced him into their lives during the war.

Wojtek, a Syrian brown bear, was relatively small for his species. Adult Syrian brown bears can reach up to 4 and a half feet in length and weigh as much as 550 pounds. Their fur, light brown in color, sometimes features a distinctive dark stripe between the shoulder blades, and they are the only bear species with white claws—a fashionable but impractical trait as it easily shows dirt.

The primary responsibility for Wojtek's care fell on two soldiers, Dymitr Szawlugo and Henryk Zacharewicz, with Henryk developing a particularly close bond with the bear. Wojtek, often seen in historical footage with Henryk, was almost like a child to him. In the wild, a Syrian brown bear's diet includes fruits, nuts, and small mammals, but the military's limited resources meant Wojtek was initially raised on condensed milk. As he grew, his diet broadened to include whatever was available, showing his adaptability rather than a discerning palate. Over time, Wojtek became a bold and familiar figure around the camp, especially near the kitchen as he searched for snacks.

In the brief respites from military duties such as packing, moving, working, or combat, Wojtek the bear eagerly engaged with his human companions. It's uncertain whether Wojtek was more of an entertainer or the entertained. Nevertheless, he was known to drink beer alongside the soldiers as one of the gang. However, unlike his human friends, Wojtek was a bear of action rather than words. As he grew larger, wrestling became one of his favorite pastimes. Although most soldiers hesitated to genuinely spar with him, the encounters typically ended with some minor injuries or torn clothes, always to the humans, never to Wojtek. Understandably, most preferred to observe these matches from a safe distance. After all, a friend who encourages wrestling with a bear might not have your best interests at heart.

Influenced by his surroundings of battle-hardened soldiers, Wojtek quickly adopted their habits. He even had his own mug for drinking beer and wine, which he would gaze at sadly when empty until someone refilled it. He also developed a taste for cigarettes, insisting they be lit before he would take them, usually consuming them in one gulp after a puff.

Upon the troops' arrival in Palestine and their incorporation into the 22nd Transport Company, Artillery Division of the Polish 2nd Corps, Wojtek was immediately embraced as the company mascot, a role that extended beyond mere symbolism. One night, a thief's attempt to steal from the camp backfired when he accidentally awakened Wojtek. The ensuing chaos alerted the soldiers, leading to the thief's capture. For his part in thwarting the theft, Wojtek was rewarded with a beer.

As Wojtek grew to weigh around 500 pounds, transporting him became more challenging. Eventually, he was assigned to one of the company's recovery trucks, akin to a military-sized tow truck used for moving tanks. This became his traveling home, where he spent his time lounging or climbing the crane for a better view of his surroundings.

Wojtek was not the only animal to accompany soldiers during the Second World War, but he was likely the only bear on the battlefield. While some animals served specific military roles, others, like Wojtek, were mascots who provided companionship. Wojtek always showed friendliness towards other animals, including Kasha the Monkey and Kirkuk the Dog, two other notable animal combatants of the war, who were considered the celebrity animals of their time.

Wojtek miraculously survived the war without sustaining any bullet or shrapnel injuries, but he did face a severe threat when he was stung on the nose by a scorpion—an injury that could have been fatal, as evidenced by his canine companion Kirkuk, who died from a similar sting. Henryk, one of Wojtek's closest human friends, was devastated and stayed by the bear's side, diligently caring for him during the critical first day and a half. Initially, it seemed Wojtek might not survive, but he resiliently overcame the scorpion's venom and soon returned to his spirited ways.

In 1943, as the 22nd Transport Company prepared for deployment to the Italian front, regulations initially barred Wojtek from joining due to a ban on animals in combat areas. However, to ensure Wojtek could stay with them, the ingenious Polish soldiers officially enlisted him in the army, complete with a paycheck, rank, and serial number. This formal enlistment not only secured his presence at the front but also documented his service under the Polish flag.

Upon reaching Italy, the Allies faced the formidable German defenses along the Winter Line. The strategic objective was to breach the line near Monte Cassino to advance towards Rome. During one of the assaults, Henryk had to advance as an artillery spotter, leaving Wojtek behind with the artillery units. Not content to remain idle, Wojtek began mimicking the soldiers by lifting and carrying heavy ammunition crates towards the guns, bravely ignoring the surrounding gunfire.

The fierce battle of Monte Cassino eventually concluded with the Allies' victory, but at a steep cost of over 70,000 lives. Following the battle, Wojtek's valiant contributions were widely celebrated, and he became a hero among his company. In tribute to his bravery, the 22nd Transport Company's emblem was redesigned to depict Wojtek carrying ammunition, a design that was then proudly displayed on their vehicles and uniforms.

After the war, the company relocated to rural Scotland, settling near the village of Hutton. As the soldiers gradually left for other postings or returned home, they each took a moment to bid farewell to Wojtek, whose story was just beginning to capture public interest. He quickly became a local celebrity, featured in media stories and visited by locals. He was even inducted into the Polish-Scottish Association.

In 1947, Wojtek retired from military service as a corporal and spent his remaining years at the Edinburgh Zoo. There, he enjoyed a tranquil life and occasional appearances on local children's shows. Despite the passage of time, he was never forgotten by his military comrades, including 82-year-old Polish veteran Augustyn Karolowski, who fondly recalled that Wojtek would still respond to his name with familiar gestures, seeking a cigarette as if still one of the boys. Wojtek lived a remarkable life filled with adventure and camaraderie, passing away in 1963 at the age of 21.

Battle of Castle Itter

On the afternoon of May 3, 1945, Zvonimir Kovic, a Yugoslavian prisoner, exited the gates of Austria's Itter Castle—a formidable fortress situated atop a hill where he was detained by Nazi SS guards—and pedaled into the dense forests beyond. Assigned to run an errand for the prison's commander, Sebastian Vimer, Kovic was a trusted maintenance man and electrician who had modified the castle into a German prison. However, this particular afternoon, Kovic harbored a secret plan; he was smuggling a note from English-speaking prisoners out of the castle, intending to deliver it to the first American soldiers he met.

Disregarding his usual routine of completing the errand and returning, Kovic opted not to head west to Vergal, a nearby city still heavily occupied by German forces, but instead embarked on a lengthy journey to Innsbruck. He traveled over 40 miles along the Inn River Valley and reached the city by evening. There, he successfully located a group from the 409th Infantry Regiment of the American 103rd Infantry Division and handed over the note. Although the unit lacked immediate authorization to initiate a rescue, they assured Kovic of a response from their headquarters by the following morning.

What unfolded next stands as one of the more remarkable and unlikely episodes of World War II—an American army commander collaborated with his adversaries, an SS captain and a Vermo major, to assemble a mixed force of American and German soldiers. Their mission led them back to the Austrian castle to liberate a group of French political prisoners, in what became known as the Battle for Castle Itter.

Castle Itter itself is perched atop a hill overlooking the village of Itter to the east, in the Austrian state of Tyrol. Positioned at the gateway to the scenic Brixen Valley, the site had hosted some form of fortress since the 11th century. The current structure of the castle was erected in 1878 on the foundations of its predecessor. In 1925, the castle was acquired by Dr. Franz Gruna, the Deputy Governor of Tyrol, who used the expansive property mainly to display his vast art and sculpture collection.

After the Anschluss in March 1938, where Austria was forcibly annexed by Nazi Germany, the country was divided into seven districts. Tyrol, along with Itter, came under the administration of a provincial Nazi government based in Vorarlberg, 990 miles to the southwest. Initially, during the early months of the German occupation, the Nazis leased Castle Itter from Dr. Gruna. At that time, the focus of the SS and the Wehrmacht—Germany's consolidated army—was primarily on quelling any traces of Austrian independence and fully integrating the country into their empire.

The German war effort was significantly bolstered by swiftly integrating young men from each conquered country into their military. Immediately following the Anschluss, the entire Austrian Army was assimilated into the Wehrmacht. While some Austrian soldiers served the Nazi cause willingly, even enthusiastically, many complied only as a means of avoiding execution. Nevertheless, small Austrian resistance groups remained active during the occupation, both in major cities like Vienna and smaller towns such as Vergo.

Despite German efforts to eliminate any Austrian soldiers deemed politically unreliable, many young Austrians who privately opposed the Nazis still found themselves conscripted into their ranks, gaining firsthand insight into Wehrmacht military strategies. Concurrently, the secretive branch of the Nazi SS, the Vafin SS, had been active in Austria since 1934, aiming to identify Austrians likely to resist the occupation. This groundwork facilitated the rounding up of dissidents, nationalists, and leftists, leading Heinrich Himmler, the SS head and one of Hitler's closest advisers, to realize the need for secure locations in Austria to detain these political prisoners temporarily before their transfer to German prisons and concentration camps.

Itter Castle's strategic location, robust walls, dry moat, and large gatehouse made it an ideal detention site. After briefly serving as a headquarters for Hitler's anti-tobacco campaign, Himmler targeted the castle for SS use. On February 7, 1943, SS Lieutenant General Oswald Po, under direct orders from Himmler, terminated the lease with the castle's owner, Dr. Gruna, seizing the property to convert it into a significant Nazi detention center. Albert Speer, Hitler's minister of armaments and war production, appointed SS Second Lieutenant Pets to supervise the conversion. Pets and his crew of 27 prisoners from Dachau and Flossenbürg camps transformed the castle into a prison, converting its guest rooms into cells and offices for SS officials and securing all potential escape routes.

By April 25, 1943, the conversion was complete, and Pets left with most of his prisoner workforce. Only two guards and an electrician, Zir Kovic, remained to finalize the modifications. Kovic, a 36-year-old Croatian electrician, had joined a Yugoslav anti-Nazi resistance group after the German invasion of Yugoslavia in April 1941 but was captured and interned in several Nazi camps before arriving at Itter. His electrical skills spared him from execution, allowing him to join the camp's maintenance crew under Pets's supervision.

Upon the prison's inauguration, its operations were placed under the authority of the Dachau concentration camp, located 90 miles northwest. SS Captain Sebastian Vimmer, known for his sadistic and unpredictable nature, took command. Vimmer, notorious for his cruelty at the Midic concentration camp in Poland, immediately implemented rigorous training for the newly formed guard force, including surprise inspections and escape drills, all of which Kovic closely observed, secretly recording details in a contraband notebook.

On May 2, 1943, Kovic witnessed the arrival of three prominent French Resistance leaders—Edward Deader, General Maurice Galon, and Leono—who were among the first high-profile prisoners brought to Itter Castle.

The newly established Itter prison housed not only Austrian dissidents and radicals but also several high-profile French detainees. These included Jean Barota, a renowned tennis star; two former Prime Ministers; three former military chiefs; and Maria Agnes Cayo, the sister of prominent French Resistance leader Charles De Gaulle. These prisoners were considered valuable to the Nazis as potential bargaining chips.

Despite varying political ideologies, the prisoners typically divided into three groups during meals to avoid conflicts. Life at Itter Castle was comparatively better than in other Nazi-controlled facilities, with adequate meals, time for exercise in the courtyard, and access to a library. The Wehrmacht guards also treated them with a notably softer approach, a disparity that grew as the war swung in favor of the Allies.

Meanwhile, the former commander of Dachau camp, Edward Vitter, had escaped to Itter Castle just before the camp's liberation. He died on May 2, 1945, under mysterious circumstances. According to former French Prime Minister Paul Reno, also a prisoner, Vitter had spent his last night drunkenly boasting of his crimes at Dachau before ultimately taking his own life.

On May 3, the French prisoners, informed by a hidden radio, learned that American forces were nearing the Tyrol area, particularly the town of Innsbruck. That afternoon, Zir Kovic left the castle on a bicycle with a secret mission to secure American aid by nightfall. Morale among the castle's guards plummeted following Vitter's mysterious death and Kovic's failure to return. Commander Vimmer, fearing for his life, fled his post, and the remaining SS guards soon deserted, leaving the prisoners in control. They armed themselves with makeshift weapons and hoisted a French flag outside the castle to signal to Allied air forces and avoid attacks.

Unable to confirm if their message had reached the Americans, the prisoners sent another emissary on May 4. They chose their Czech cook, Andreas Kobit, who rode to the recently liberated town of Vergal on a guard's bicycle with another note. Vergal had been abandoned by demoralized Wehrmacht forces, though SS patrols still threatened the area. Kobit successfully met with the Austrian resistance and their commander, Major Ysf Gengle. A former Wehrmacht officer disillusioned with the Nazis, Gengle had severed ties with the German Army and was leading the local resistance, having armed them with Wehrmacht supplies—a capital offense.

By the time Kobit reached him, Gengle was already aware of the situation at the castle. Though he considered a rescue mission, he couldn't leave Vergal unprotected or risk the castle falling to an SS counterattack. Instead, Gengle drove to the nearby town of Kin, 8 miles north, where he met with Captain Lee, the 27-year-old commander of the 23rd Tank Battalion, 12th Armored Division. Displaying a white flag, Gengle informed Lee of the castle's plight. Lee, expecting Kin to be his final assignment before the war's end, quickly agreed to lead a rescue mission and contacted his superiors for approval.

Lee realized he lacked sufficient vehicles to escort all the prisoners from the castle to Kin safely. Instead, he planned to fortify the castle against SS attacks until reinforcements from the 142nd Battalion could arrive to eliminate the SS threat in the area. Accompanied by Gengle, Lee drove to the castle in Gengle's military vehicle, followed by reinforcements from Lee's tank division. However, they had to turn back at a bridge that seemed too fragile to bear their weight.

Fourteen American soldiers from Lee's division, along with a driver and ten former Wehrmacht riflemen, continued towards the castle. When they were about four miles from the castle gates, they encountered a group of SS troops setting up a roadblock. A firefight ensued, but Lee's group prevailed and retreated to the castle for safety.

Inside, the prisoners had enlisted the help of Kurt Siegfried Schader, an SS officer at the prison who had defected from the Nazi cause, to lead the castle's defense. Sensing an impending SS attack, Lee and Gengle assessed the situation upon arrival. They found an unusual alliance of German defectors, French political prisoners, and Austrian resistance members united under Schader's command.

To distinguish friendly German troops from enemy combatants, those inside the castle were instructed to wear strips of black cloth around their arms. The SS troops soon surrounded the castle, probing for vulnerabilities rather than launching an immediate attack. The potential for being executed for treason loomed over the defectors if the SS overcame them, and one German soldier, panicking, fled over the castle walls into the forest.

This incident raised concerns about the reliability of the remaining German soldiers, but Gengle convinced Lee to let them keep their weapons. From the top level of the keep, Lee, Gengle, and Schader observed over a hundred SS troops setting up artillery in the surrounding woods. Using a telephone, Gengle contacted his fellow resistance leader in Virgle, Aloi Mayer, to warn of the heavy SS presence and to request additional reinforcements.

As the battle commenced at 10 a.m., Lee's personal tank, nicknamed "Bastion Jenny," was positioned defensively at the castle's main gate. Despite taking heavy fire from an SS gun, the three men assigned to it survived and retreated into the castle. The question became how long they could sustain their defense, relying on the castle's structure. If the SS breached the exterior walls, they planned to retreat to the central armored keep for a strategic defense. Women and children were sheltered in the cellar, while some men stayed above ground to protect it.

Aware that the 142nd Division lacked a full understanding of the enemy's strength and unable to communicate due to his downed tank radio, Captain Lee needed to inform the approaching reinforcements quickly. Jean Botra, the famous tennis star, volunteered to deliver the message. Using his agility, Botra scaled the castle walls and navigated through SS positions to reach the 142nd Battalion, briefing them on the situation before requesting an American uniform to join them as they marched back to the castle.

The relief force arrived at the castle at 4 p.m., and with their assistance, the remaining SS forces were swiftly subdued, capturing over a hundred SS soldiers. The French prisoners were evacuated that evening, safely returning to Paris by May 10th. Just two days later, Germany signed its unconditional surrender, marking the end of the European theater of World War II. The exact number of casualties from the battle remains unknown, but several Wehrmacht defectors were either injured or killed by SS fire while aiding the resistance. Gengle died during the battle from a sniper bullet while trying to protect French Prime Minister Reno. Honored posthumously as an Austrian national hero, a street in Virgle was named in his memory.

Charles VI, The Glass King

Charles VI was born in 1368, amid the longest conflict in European history, the Hundred Years' War. He became known by two nicknames, Charles the Beloved and Charles the Mad, reflecting the dual aspects of his reign. His rule was marred by frequent bouts of mental illness, during one of which he believed he was made of glass. This led him to wear reinforced clothing and to avoid physical contact with others. His condition was so severe and puzzling that his doctors resorted to drilling into his skull, seeking a cure for his strange and unprecedented disease.

The exploration extends into the captivating realm of 14th century France, the era of the last jewel, the setting for Shakespeare's historical plays, and the reign of a much-maligned monarch who ceded his kingdom to the English. To comprehend his life, it is essential to grasp the devastating dynastic conflicts between the royal houses of England and France, embodied in the Hundred Years' War, and the catastrophic effects of the Black Death, which together reduced France's population by half.

After the Norman invasion of England in 1066, French kings occupied the English throne. They spoke French, enacted French laws, married French women, and granted English lands to French nobles while still maintaining extensive territories in France. Although they ruled England, their holdings in France made them vassals to the French king, a relationship they reluctantly maintained. The French crown, uneasy with such a powerful neighbor, gradually eroded the historically English territories. By 1337, only Gascony remained under English control. When the French crown attempted to annex Gascony as well, Edward III of England invaded, aiming to claim the French throne himself.

Following the English successes at Crécy and Poitiers, a freak hailstorm devastated Edward's army, forcing him to abandon his claim in exchange for more land in Gascony. After a brief peace, Charles V, the father of Charles VI and known as Charles the Mad, revitalized the French state and military, reclaiming most of the English-held territories. His untimely death at 42 left the throne to his 11-year-old son, Charles VI.

Charles VI's youth under the regency of his self-interested uncles left him free to pursue his passions for hunting and jousting. Married at 16 to Isabel of Bavaria, who bore him 12 children, Charles was described by chroniclers as lusty, with a robust carnal appetite. By 20, the regency ended, but Charles left state administration to his father's former advisers, focusing instead on his personal pursuits.

At 23, Charles experienced his first severe mental health episode while trying to negotiate peace with England in Amiens. He suffered from high fevers, delirium, and, unusually, hair and nail loss, leading some to suggest he might have had sarcoidosis. However, the simultaneous illness of other courtiers suggests an infectious disease, likely typhoid fever, which can cause nail loss in severe cases.

After recovering sufficiently to resume hunting, tragedy struck when one of his closest advisers was attacked and nearly killed. The assailant fled to the Duke of Brittany, an old adversary of the king. Enraged, Charles wanted immediate military retribution, despite still suffering from intermittent fevers and not being fully mentally recovered. Ignoring his physicians' advice, he led his army in the summer of 1392, during one of the hottest summers on record, which exacerbated widespread crop failures and livestock deaths.

Progress was excruciatingly slow, which led to his heightened impatience. Chronicles depict him as behaving irrationally, uttering nonsensical phrases and making wild gestures. As Charles and his entourage journeyed through a forest near Le Mans, a disheveled man emerged, seized the king's horse's bridle, and shouted, "Ride no further, noble king! Turn back; you are betrayed!" Although the king's guards pushed the man away, they did not detain him, and he continued to follow the group for half an hour, repeating his warning, which disturbed the king.

Upon leaving the forest and entering the glaring midday sun of an open plain, a sudden noise—a page dropping the king's lance, which clanged against a helmet—startled Charles. Mistaking his companions for foes, he drew his sword and charged, leading to a chaotic skirmish until his exhaustion caused him to collapse.

In his frenzied state, he inadvertently killed a knight and several others. For the next two days, he was barely coherent, speaking incoherently. His physician, the 92-year-old Guillaume de Jacini, attributed his condition to an excess of maternal moisture, referencing his mother's severe postnatal depression. He recommended rest, good nutrition, and hydration, a diagnosis reflecting the ancient Greek humoral theory, which posited that health stemmed from a balance of four bodily humors: blood, yellow bile, black bile, and phlegm.

Seizing the opportunity during Charles's recovery, his uncles once again usurped power. At a masquerade ball in 1393, known as the Ball of the Burning Men, a tragic accident occurred when a guest's costume caught fire, rapidly spreading flames. The Duchess saved the king by smothering the fire with her gown, but four men perished and others suffered severe burns.

Months later, Charles exhibited inappropriate behavior and violence, shadowed heavily when his wife visited. He inquired about her identity and instructed his servants to fulfill her needs so she would leave him be. He claimed he was unmarried, childless, not the king of France, and not named Charles. He even defaced his and his wife's coat of arms. Though often described in historical texts as memory loss or non-recognition of his wife, it seemed more akin to nihilistic delusions associated with severe depression.

Eventually, his physicians performed a trepanning, drilling into his skull—a procedure common in prehistoric Europe but rare in his time. Whether due to his doctors' interventions or the natural progression of his illness, Charles improved. After six months, he expressed his gratitude for his recovery at Mont Saint Michel.

However, further episodes persisted. In 1395, he claimed he was not a king, insisted his real name was Georges, and once again defaced his royal coat of arms. He would often dash through the corridors of his Parisian residence, the Hôtel Saint Paul, screaming that he was fleeing from his enemies. To prevent him from escaping, the entrances were sealed.

After several months, he expressed his gratitude for his recovery at the Notre Dame Cathedral.

In the initial stages of a relapse the following year, he requested that his dagger be removed, along with those of his courtiers. This indicated his awareness of his deteriorating condition and his ability to take sensible measures before succumbing to madness once more. When lucid, he participated in state affairs, but these periods of clarity became increasingly brief. During his episodes, he could become feverish and erratic, engaging in bizarre behaviors like breaking objects, throwing valuables into the fire, and damaging clothing. Sometimes, he was utterly lethargic, neglecting personal hygiene for months, which led to skin issues and body lice.

Various causes were proposed for the king's illness, including poisoning, sorcery, witchcraft, and demonic possession, and the treatments attempted were equally varied. He underwent exorcisms, isolated prayer, diaphoretic medications to induce sweating, and even powdered pearls. In 1405, an early form of shock treatment was tried; ten men with blackened faces startled him, which surprisingly prompted him to resume washing.

His relationship with his wife deteriorated, fueled by rumors of her infidelity with his brother, the Duke of Orleans. She arranged for a pleasant young woman, referred to as the "little queen," to comfort him. Their relationship broke down entirely in 1417 when he commanded her to close her lively and reputedly decadent court at the Hôtel Barbette.

The king's later psychotic episodes were less documented, but Pope Pius II noted in his commentaries that Charles sometimes believed he was made of glass, taking measures like incorporating iron rods into his clothing to prevent shattering, and avoiding physical contact.

The glass delusion, though bizarre, was not uncommon in Europe at that time, with numerous accounts of individuals fearing they had fragile glass bodies.

The king's illness created a power vacuum, leading to conflicts among his uncles, his wife, and his brother Louis, plunging France into civil strife. This internal turmoil, coupled with his vulnerability, allowed Henry V of England to invade and decisively defeat the French at Agincourt in 1415.

Charles was compelled to sign a treaty that disinherited his son and declared Henry V regent and heir to the French throne. Charles VI succumbed to quartan fever, believed to be malaria, in the summer of 1422. His death came just weeks after Henry V's, whose infant son, also Charles's grandson, then ascended to the thrones of England and France as Henry VI. Like his grandfather, Henry VI suffered from mental illness, which allowed Charles's disinherited son, the Dauphin, aided by Joan of Arc, to challenge English rule. He was eventually crowned King Charles VII, known as Charles the Victorious, and led France to end the Hundred Years' War in 1453.

Boston Molasses Flood of 1919

Around 12:30 PM on January 15, 1919, in the North End neighborhood of Boston, Massachusetts, a massive storage tank filled with molasses burst. The resulting flood of molasses swept through the streets at high speed, destroying buildings, lifting vehicles, and engulfing unsuspecting individuals. In a short span, the Boston Molasses Flood claimed 21 lives.

Molasses was widely used in 1919, primarily for fermenting into ethanol, an essential component in both alcoholic beverages and munitions. The Purity Distilling Company, located at 529 Commercial Street, managed the unloading, storage, and processing of large molasses shipments from incoming ships. The tank responsible for the disaster stood 15 meters tall and 27 meters in diameter, capable of holding over 2 million gallons of molasses.

When the tank collapsed, it released these two million gallons almost instantaneously, creating a destructive wave of molasses that moved at speeds up to 56 kilometers per hour (about 35 miles per hour) and reached the height of a two-story building. This wave was so powerful that it lifted a streetcar off its elevated track, flattened some buildings, and dislodged others from their foundations.

Many victims were immediately overwhelmed by the flood, but the danger persisted even after the wave subsided. The molasses, denser than water, settled waist-deep in the streets. As it cooled in the open air, it thickened, making escape increasingly difficult.

An eyewitness described the scene as chaotic, with both animals and people struggling to move in the viscous molasses. The resemblance to flies caught on flypaper was noted, as the more they struggled, the more ensnared they became.

A desperate rescue operation ensued, with rescuers working tirelessly to extract survivors from the molasses before they suffocated. This laborious effort continued for four days until it transitioned into a cleanup operation. Some victims, covered in molasses or washed into the harbor, were not identified for months.

To clean up the aftermath, crews used saltwater to dissolve the molasses and sand to absorb it. Despite the assistance of hundreds of volunteers, the cleanup was prolonged by the sticky residue that people carried with them outside the flood area.

Streetcars, telephones, benches, and subway platforms many blocks from the disaster site remained sticky with molasses for weeks following the event. This incident led to one of the first class action lawsuits in Massachusetts, initiated by local residents. Initially, the Purity Distilling Company attributed the tank's explosion to anarchists, denying responsibility for the flood. However, they retracted this claim when overwhelming evidence was presented, eventually compensating victims with approximately $7,000 each, an amount equivalent to about $100,000 today.

An investigation after the disaster found the tank was only half as thick as necessary and was partly made of brittle manganese. No basic safety tests had been conducted during its construction, and multiple warning signs had been disregarded. Notably, the tank emitted loud groans when filled and leaked so severely that locals would collect molasses from it. Instead of fixing these leaks, management had the tank painted brown to better conceal them.

The cause of the disaster was determined to be thermal expansion. A batch of warm molasses added the previous day had raised the temperature and volume of the tank's contents, and slightly warmer weather contributed to the tank's rupture.

Today, the site where the tank once stood is now a baseball diamond in a public park. The park is a place for recreation and features a small plaque commemorating the victims of this unusual disaster. Some say that the smell of molasses can still be detected in Boston's North End.

Caligula's Horse Incitatus

Acquiring the celebrated horse Incitatus marked a pivotal moment in the life of Caligula, the Roman Emperor noted for his eventful and lavish reign. This horse introduced an unprecedented level of eccentricity and flamboyance to Caligula's inner circle. Believed to have been acquired around 39 AD, Incitatus quickly became a cherished member of the imperial court. As a thoroughbred that captured the emperor's attention, Incitatus was treated in a uniquely extravagant manner from the outset.

According to historical accounts, Incitatus lived in a marble stable, an unheard-of luxury for an animal at the time, and its diet was meticulously managed, consisting of the finest grains and fodder. The horse was also bestowed with senatorial status and enjoyed noble privileges, including an ivory trough and meals served in silver dishes. Caligula even adorned Incitatus with purple, a color traditionally associated with royalty, and arranged for the horse to be covered in this regal hue.

Further historical insights reveal that Incitatus not only enjoyed material comforts but also held the title of priest. The horse had a vast retinue of slaves, personal guards, and even its own ceremonial form. Caligula often personally invited Incitatus to dine with him, offering barley and wine from a golden cup.

Despite being a horse, Incitatus is a complex and somewhat elusive figure in history. It's challenging to determine the exact extent of his influence on Roman politics as a senator. Historians remain divided over this issue; although Incitatus never achieved the position of Consul as Caligula might have wished, the historical narratives about him are contentious. Scholars argue that Roman chroniclers like Suetonius and Cassius Dio may have faced political pressures to depict Emperor Caligula negatively, potentially skewing the facts to fit the agendas of subsequent emperors.

Some suggest that Caligula's promotion of Incitatus might have been a satirical act meant to mock the Roman Senate. Whether true or not, the story certainly focused attention on the emperor, leading many to view him as both bizarre and extravagant.

The Carrington Event

On the evening of August 28, 1859, a luminous spectacle unfolded across global skies. In some regions, the sky burned a deep red, mimicking the glow of a colossal wildfire, while in others, wide swathes of white light pirouetted through the darkness. This phenomenon persisted for nearly a week, illuminating the night so intensely that newspapers could be read at midnight without additional light.

Throughout the world, people congregated outdoors, simultaneously terrified and mesmerized. The vast majority were clueless about the cause, speculating it might signal the apocalypse.

Reports from various countries described the extraordinary events following that night. In Boston, the sky radiated a fiery red, convincing many of an unseen blaze on the horizon, until the color shifted to a stark green. Observers elsewhere noted columns of light traversing the heavens, with multi-hued rays and arches dynamically forming and dissipating.

An article in the San Francisco Herald described the scene vividly: "The entire sky seemed to ripple like a wheat field in a strong breeze. The Bay's waters mirrored the aurora's vibrant colors. The spectacle was overwhelmingly magnificent and viewed by thousands with a blend of astonishment and pleasure."

The brilliance was so intense that some people mistook it for dawn. In South

Carolina, a group of masons began their day's work early, only to realize the actual time and return home. In Virginia, a railroad conductor, irritated by larks chirping as if morning had broken, shot three birds to silence them and return to sleep.

In Ohio, the sight of a night sky lit up like a festive display overwhelmed a 16-year-old girl. Overwhelmed by the celestial anomaly, she spiraled into panic, convinced it heralded the end of the world, and was eventually institutionalized.

As awe and fear gripped the public, telegraph operators worldwide faced strange malfunctions. Some experienced shocks and burns from their equipment, which emitted unexpected sparks and arcs. Remarkably, operators found they could continue sending messages even after disconnecting their power sources. Between Boston and Portland, telegraphers, initially amazed by their battery-less capability, continued their routine operations.

Throughout that week, newspapers were replete with stories of the celestial dazzle and the peculiar disruptions within the telegraph system.

In some instances, the only news that could be published was local because disruptions in telegraph services halted incoming international news dispatches.

Overall, these occurrences seemed inexplicable, leading many to suspect they were omens of an impending apocalypse. However, the true cause was far less dramatic and would later be revealed through the findings of Richard Carrington, a British amateur astronomer. On September 1, 1859, from his private observatory on his estate outside London, Carrington was meticulously observing sunspots—dark, transient phenomena on the sun's surface which he believed were crucial to understand.

During his observations, Carrington noticed an anomaly: two bright white spots flared up on the sun's surface and then vanished. Curious, he documented this event with a sketch that he later submitted to the Royal Astronomical Society as part of a detailed report.

Unbeknownst to him at the time, Carrington had observed a pair of solar flares—intense explosions on the sun's surface that often eject substantial amounts of energetic particles. While the sun continually emits a solar wind of such particles, Earth's magnetic field usually shields us from their harmful effects and atmospheric degradation. Only a small fraction of these particles penetrates our atmosphere, primarily at the poles, causing the Aurora Borealis or Northern Lights. However, during solar flares, the sun expels a significantly larger volume of magnetized plasma. If Earth is in the path of this plasma, the Aurora Borealis can be seen much further from the poles.

The flares Carrington observed had propelled a massive surge of magnetized plasma toward Earth. That evening, the mesmerizing celestial lights reappeared globally. It would take some time before Carrington's observations connected these spectacular skies to the solar flares. Once made, this connection led to naming the phenomenon after him: the Carrington Event.

Carrington would likely have been honored by this recognition. The Carrington Event, while it disrupted communications, was not lethal. At the time, it appeared as a peculiar yet significant scientific milestone, not posing any severe threat to humanity.

The significance of the Carrington Event cannot be overlooked. In 1859, the only major technology that depended on electricity was the telegraph system. Today, however, our entire infrastructure relies heavily on electrical power, raising a critical question: what would the consequences be if a Carrington-level event occurred in the present day?

Unlike in 1859, we would likely receive some advance warning of an impending geomagnetic storm, with systems in place to provide at least a day's notice. The extent of the storm's impact would hinge greatly on our preparedness. A swift, coordinated effort to temporarily shut down vulnerable systems could mitigate damage, limiting global disruptions to about a week in an ideal scenario.

Conversely, the worst-case scenario—lacking adequate preparation or warning—could lead to unprecedented widespread blackouts, disrupting power, communications, and most modern technology simultaneously.

This scenario would see planes grounded, hospitals without power, and city traffic controls non-operational. Card transactions would cease, refrigeration systems would fail, banking services would be disrupted, and supply chains would collapse. The technological setback could resemble regressing several centuries, and not just temporarily. If power grids are not preemptively taken offline, the damage could be long-lasting. Experts suggest that recovering from such extensive damage could take up to a decade.

Moreover, it's a matter of when, not if, another Carrington-level event will occur. While estimates vary, some scientists believe such events could hit Earth approximately every 150 years. Since more than 160 years have passed since the last event, we might already be overdue for another.

Switzerland Invades Liechtenstein

Switzerland is known for its consistent neutrality in conflicts, most notably during World War II, similar to Ireland—though Ireland arguably had less at stake historically. However, Switzerland's neutrality has not been without blemishes. They have inadvertently invaded Liechtenstein three times and even bombed it. So, how did these mishaps occur? Many might wonder, "What exactly is Liechtenstein?" It's not a bizarre act from a German nightclub, but a small principality nestled between Switzerland and Austria. Established in 1719 under the Holy Roman Empire, it is ruled by the House of Liechtenstein, with the Prince as its head of state. It's the fourth smallest country in Europe, covering only 160 square kilometers, and has a population of over 30,000. It is doubly landlocked, with both itself and all neighboring countries lacking a coastline.

Switzerland and Liechtenstein share a unique bond. Despite being a sovereign state, Liechtenstein could easily be mistaken for part of Switzerland. They share a currency, language, and have an open border policy. Liechtenstein has no military, so Switzerland acts as its protector, akin to an older sibling. Switzerland even handles international representation and treaty negotiations for Liechtenstein. Their relationship is endearing, setting an example for neighborly peace, though it has experienced strain due to Switzerland's accidental military actions. One notable incident occurred on October 14, 1968, when the Swiss army accidentally fired explosives into a Liechtenstein ski resort—an unusual error for a nation more commonly associated with the precision of a Swiss Army knife.

Fortunately, no one was injured at the ski resort, although I can't say the same for my culinary escapades. The first accidental Swiss incursion into Liechtenstein occurred in 1976 when over 70 Swiss soldiers and their 50 horses mistakenly ventured half a kilometer into Liechtenstein. The locals found the situation amusing and even offered the troops drinks, though the Swiss soldiers found it quite embarrassing and quickly departed.

A more serious incident occurred when Swiss rockets were mistakenly launched into a Liechtenstein forest, sparking a significant fire and causing extensive damage. The Swiss attributed the error to adverse weather conditions and compensated with millions of francs for the damages.

In 1992, another inadvertent invasion took place when Swiss army cadets were instructed to establish an observation post in the village of Triesenberg. The alarmed locals were puzzled by the presence of a foreign military in full combat gear. It turned out that the Swiss Command had overlooked the fact that Triesenberg was not in Switzerland. An apology was issued after the troops withdrew.

The most recent misstep happened in 2007 when about 170 Swiss troops mistakenly entered Liechtenstein under poor weather conditions. They quickly retreated upon realizing the mistake, and when Switzerland apologized, Liechtenstein responded that they hadn't even noticed the intrusion.

Thus, the tale of Switzerland as the unintended aggressor of Liechtenstein unfolds, with each incident chalked up as an accident. However, one might argue that repeating the same mistake more than once stretches the definition of an "accident."

Interestingly, apart from the forest fire, Liechtenstein has always been forgiving towards these gaffes, maintaining a good-natured demeanor. In a quirky historical footnote, the last time Liechtenstein deployed an army was during the Austro-Prussian War of 1866. They sent out 80 men and not only did they suffer no casualties, they actually returned with 81, having made a new friend along the way.

53

Oliver Cromwell's Head

Oliver Cromwell was one of the most controversial figures in British history. He led Parliament's army, the New Model Army, during the English Civil War against King Charles I, who was widely regarded as a tyrant. Cromwell's forces ultimately triumphed over the Royalists, culminating in one of the most infamous events in English history: the execution of Charles I. On a dreary morning in late January 1649, the king was led to a scaffold outside the Banqueting House in London and executed before a large crowd.

This decision was not universally popular, and it led to a period without a monarchy, and Cromwell assuming the role of Lord Protector. Following his death, however, the monarchy was restored. Cromwell himself was subjected to posthumous disgrace. Today, we explore the posthumous execution of Oliver Cromwell.

Cromwell reigned as Lord Protector from December 1653 until his death five years later. Although Parliament offered him the crown, Cromwell instead chose to remain a guardian or protector of the Commonwealth. He pondered over the offer for six weeks before declining, opting instead to be ceremonially reinstalled as Lord Protector in an event reminiscent of a coronation, with his powers clearly defined by legislation.

Throughout 1658, Cromwell battled various illnesses, suffering from malarial fever and kidney issues. The death of his daughter, Elizabeth Claypole, in

August 1658, likely accelerated his decline. Cromwell died at the age of 59 at Whitehall on September 3rd, most likely from blood poisoning caused by a urinary infection. His funeral, marked by grandeur and ceremony, mirrored that of King James I. Cromwell was buried in the newly created Henry VII Chapel at Westminster Abbey, with honors akin to those of a monarch.

Cromwell's body remained undisturbed in the chapel at Westminster Abbey until the restoration of the monarchy. Upon his ascension, Charles II, son of Charles I, sought retribution against those involved in his father's execution. Fifty-nine commissioners, or regicides, who had signed the death warrant were targeted, but many had already passed away. Of the regicides brought to trial, the 12 surviving signatories were hanged, drawn, and quartered. Moreover, it was decreed that those already deceased would be subjected to posthumous execution.

During this period, the remains of traitors were considered property of the crown, with their heads often displayed in public areas like Tower Bridge or above the Palace of Westminster. Efforts were made to exhume Cromwell's body, which was hidden in the wall of Westminster Abbey's middle aisle. The exhumation was challenging due to the wooden enclosures, but was eventually accomplished.

On January 28, 1661, the bodies of Oliver Cromwell, John Bradshaw, and Henry Ireton were unearthed and taken to the Red Lion Inn in Holborn. Two days later, on the anniversary of Charles I's execution, their bodies were paraded through London's streets on sledges to Tyburn, the notorious execution site. Here, the bodies were hanged in chains from the triangular gallows until the late afternoon, presenting a grisly and unsettling spectacle.

Following the hanging, the decaying bodies were taken down for beheading. Cromwell's body required eight axe blows to sever the head, which was then displayed before the crowd and spiked above Westminster Hall. The fate of Cromwell's remains has since intrigued historians, with various theories circulating. One rumor suggests that his daughter Mary retrieved his body from Tyburn and secretly interred it at Newburgh Priory, where a sealed stone vault purportedly contains the remains of the headless Cromwell.

However, generations of the family have consistently refused requests to open the vault, even denying a petition from King Edward VII. Other theories suggest that Cromwell's body remained in the pit at Tyburn, with no attempt made to retrieve it. Cromwell's head remained on a spike above Westminster Hall until the late 1680s. It eventually came into private ownership after a storm during the reign of James II caused the pole to snap, sending the head tumbling to the ground. It was then picked up and reportedly hidden in the chimney of a house. At the time, rewards were offered for Cromwell's head due to its symbolic significance.

The head later surfaced in a London freak show at Dupoy's Museum, mis-labeled as the "monster's head." Over the years, the head changed hands multiple times, each exchange increasing its perceived value. Finally, in 1960, Cromwell's head was donated to his alma mater, Sidney Sussex College, where it was buried in a dignified yet secretive manner within the college grounds.

Oliver Cromwell remains a highly divisive figure in English history. The treatment of his body after death—both shocking and captivating—illustrates the intense quest for possession of the head of one of Britain's most polarizing figures. This also reflects the disdain held for him following the restoration of Charles II. The spectacle of his posthumous execution would have been an extraordinary and disturbing event for the spectators in London.

The Beer Flood of 1814

On October 17, 1814, a massive wooden vat containing fermenting beer ruptured at the Horseshoe Brewery in London. This incident released over 1 million liters (approximately 260,000 U.S. gallons) of beer, inundating the streets of a poor neighborhood with disastrous effects. The aroma of beer lingered in the area for months following the spill, which prompted significant reforms in London's brewing industry.

Sir Henry Muse, who was deeply rooted in the brewing sector, learned the trade from his father, Richard Muse, who owned a prosperous brewery in London. In 1795, Richard constructed the largest vat ever made at the time, holding 20,000 barrels and costing £10,000. After a disagreement with his father in 1809, Sir Henry struck out on his own and acquired the Horseshoe Brewery, renaming it Henry Muse and Company. Situated at the junction of Tottenham Court Road and Oxford Street—now a prime shopping location in the UK—the brewery was once nestled in a labyrinth of narrow streets and cramped alleys populated by impoverished residents, often referred to as "Little Ireland" due to the high concentration of Irish immigrants.

When Charles Dickens visited in the early 19th century, he remarked on the dire conditions: the streets were too narrow and the houses too small to ever be considered desirable dwellings. The area, which inspired William Hogarth's "Gin Lane," a depiction of starvation, madness, and infanticide, was one of the city's poorest locales.

The Henry Muse and Company Brewery specialized in porter, a dark brown beer favored by the porters working at London's docks. Sir Henry's brew became highly popular, and by 1811, his brewery was producing over 100,000 barrels annually, making it the sixth largest porter brewery in London.

Riding high on their success, Muse and Company merged with the Klausen Company Brewery in southeast London, initiating an expansion across the city. At that time, constructing enormous vats was a notable feat that ambitious breweries often undertook, especially those that produced Porter, which typically involved several large vats on site. Some of these vats stood over six meters (20 feet) tall, reinforced by hefty iron bands, each weighing about 320 kilograms (700 pounds).

On the afternoon of October 17, 1814, George Crick, the storehouse clerk at the brewery, was conducting routine checks when he noticed a slipped iron band on one of the vats. Although this was a common issue and not initially a cause for concern, he reported it to his supervisor. He was reassured there was no immediate danger and instructed to write to Florence Young, a brewery partner, to arrange for repairs. The vat in question was 6.7 meters (22 feet) tall, weighed approximately 33,000 kilograms (33 tons), and contained about 580,000 liters (154,000 U.S. gallons) of beer.

At 5:30 PM, the displaced iron band completely detached, causing the enormous vat to rupture and flood the brewery. This event triggered other barrels to burst, adding to the deluge. Reports suggest the total spillage reached about 1.5 million liters (400,000 U.S. gallons).

George Crick later recounted the incident, noting he was just 30 feet away when the vat exploded. He described the scene as one of "dreadful devasta-tion," with the force knocking over barrels and breaching the brewery's walls, which were two and a half bricks thick.

The ensuing wave of beer wreaked havoc, crashing through the wall of the adjacent Tavistock Arms Pub, where 14-year-old Eleanor Cooper was working. Tragically, she was killed by the debris while washing pots, becoming the flood's first victim. The beer then surged into New Street, a cul-de-sac with poor drainage, creating a wave 4.6 meters (15 feet) high that demolished two houses.

In one of the destroyed houses, four-year-old Hannah Bamfield was having tea with her mother when the wave swept them into the street, killing Hannah instantly. Simultaneously, a wake for a two-year-old boy in the basement of another house was catastrophically interrupted, resulting in the deaths of all five mourners: 60-year-old Anne Savile, 30-year-old Mary Malvey, three-year-old Thomas Murray, 27-year-old Elizabeth Smith, and 65-year-old Catherine Butler.

The flat and low-lying terrain around the brewery, combined with inadequate drainage, caused the beer to flood into numerous cellars and basements. Residents were forced to seek refuge on higher floors or furniture to escape the rising tide of Porter. Tragically, three-year-old Sarah Bates could not be rescued and also perished in the flood.

The Morning Post later described the scene as a "desolate vista, so dreadful it could be likened to the aftermath of a fire or earthquake." At the brewery, the flood reached waist-high, and workers were extricated from the debris by a large crowd that had gathered to assist. Some brewery employees were hospitalized, but fortunately, no workers perished due to the incident.

In the days following the disaster, rumors circulated about additional fatalities caused by locals excessively consuming the spilled beer. However, contemporary reports contradicted these claims, highlighting the calm and concerted efforts in the rescue operations, with people remaining quiet to better hear those trapped in cellars.

After the rescue operations concluded, hundreds visited the site to view the shattered vats and the devastation left behind. The brewery began charging for entry to the premises, while families of the deceased displayed their loved ones' bodies in a nearby yard, inviting public donations for funeral expenses.

The flood inflicted severe damage, destroying two houses and claiming eight lives. A coroner's inquest, overseen by George Harrison and convened two days post-disaster, involved inspections and testimonies, including from George Crick and the landlord of the adjacent Tavistock Arms Pub. The jury declared the incident an "act of God," attributing the deaths to accidental misfortune.

This verdict did not satisfy all, including an anonymous Morning Post contributor who argued that breweries and distilleries posed significant risks in populous areas. The inquiry concluded without requiring the brewery to compensate the victims' families. Nonetheless, Henry Muse and Company faced about £23,000 in losses, including the beer and physical damages. Financial ruin was narrowly averted when Parliament allowed the brewery to reclaim excise duty on the lost beer, granting them £7,250.

A public collection for the victims' families raised £33 to cover burial costs. The Horseshoe Brewery continued operations until its closure in 1921, demolished a year later to make way for the Dominion Theatre, which still operates on Tottenham Court Road today. Following this tragedy, the brewing industry gradually transitioned from wooden to concrete vats, ensuring such a disaster would not recur.

Mike the Headless Chicken

On the morning of September 10, 1945, while beheading chickens on his family's farm in Fruita, Colorado, Lloyd Olsen was startled to see one of the birds start running around the yard after its head had been chopped off. Placing the bird, now named Mike, in a box, Olsen expected it would not survive the night. To his surprise, Mike was alive the next morning. Sensing a unique opportunity, Olsen took Mike along to town, where he planned to sell farm produce. In town, Olsen visited the local tavern, showcasing Mike to incredulous patrons and betting them a beer that Mike was indeed a live, headless chicken. Many took the wager, allowing Olsen to drink for free. However, this local spectacle was just the beginning of what would become far greater fame and financial success over the following 18 months.

Before delving into Mike's extraordinary survival, it's crucial to understand the biological factors at play. A critical blood clot prevented Mike from bleeding out as the axe had missed his jugular vein, leaving most of his brainstem and one ear intact. This enabled Mike to retain vital functions like breathing and heart rate, thanks to his brainstem which governs basic bodily processes. Furthermore, chickens have a secondary balance mechanism in their pelvic area known as the lumbosacral organ, which suggests that the brain's vestibular system isn't solely responsible for balance and walking. Thus, despite losing about 90% of his head, the remaining 10% of Mike's brain was sufficient for him to perform basic movements. The intact portion of his trachea allowed him to breathe and eat, and the fortuitous blood clot enabled his survival after the initial injury. Olsen meticulously cared for Mike, feeding him a mixture of milk and water via eyedropper, and supplementing with cornmeal and worms, demonstrating remarkable adaptability and care.

With Lloyd Olsen's care, Mike managed to lead a somewhat normal bird life despite his unique condition. He engaged in typical chicken behaviors like pecking at the ground and trying to preen his feathers, though his attempts to crow produced only gurgling noises. Initially just a curiosity, Mike's story caught the public's interest and was first reported in a local newspaper. It soon garnered wider attention, earning him the nickname Miracle Mike, and caught the eye of a sideshow promoter from Salt Lake City, Utah, named Hope Wade.

Under Wade's guidance, the Olsens and Mike embarked on a nationwide tour, making headlines in major publications like Time and Life magazines. Mike became an international sensation, receiving fan mail from all over the world, and was displayed for an admission fee of 25 cents. At the peak of his fame, the Olsens earned $4,500 a month from his appearances—equivalent to over $54,000 today. Mike was also insured for $10,000, now worth over $120,000.

Tragically, Mike's life came to an end in Phoenix, Arizona, during a sideshow event when his airway became blocked and the Olsens could not find the eyedropper needed to clear his trachea. After an extraordinary 18 months of survival, Mike died on March 17, 1947.

Mike's legacy continues to thrive in Fruita, Colorado, where the annual Mike the Headless Chicken Festival is held every third weekend in May. The festival kicks off on a Thursday with a city-hosted event and spans the weekend with a variety of activities. Friday sees tents set up at the Fruita Civic Center with late-night performances, local restaurants bustling, and family-friendly activities like corn hole and hoverboard rides. The main attractions unfold on Saturday with the Mike the Headless Chicken 5K race, renowned for its beautiful route and competitive spirit, and a disc golf tournament at Snooks

Bottom, which offers a unique course alongside the Colorado River. The festival also features craft stalls from local vendors, a car show, and a poultry exhibition showcasing over a hundred rare and unusual birds. The event concludes with a wing eating contest and live music, ensuring Mike's spirited legacy endures as a celebration of his improbable survival and the community he inspired. If you're ever near Fruita, consider visiting this festival to pay tribute to the little chicken that captured the hearts of many.

Project A119

On October 4, 1957, the Soviet Union captured a significant lead in the Space Race by launching Sputnik 1, the first artificial satellite, into orbit. This event triggered the Sputnik crisis in the United States, where the public was significantly unsettled by the USSR's advanced technological capabilities. The concern was not merely about the Soviet lead in aerospace science; the real worry was the newfound vulnerability of the US to potential Soviet missile strikes. At the time, the US was planning to launch its own satellite using a rocket capable of producing 150,000 pounds (670,000 Newtons) of thrust, which limited the satellite's weight to approximately 21.5 pounds (under 10 kilograms). In contrast, Sputnik weighed a substantial 184 pounds (83 kilograms), supported by the Soviet R7 rocket's impressive one million pounds (4.4 million Newtons) of thrust. This capability suggested that the USSR could develop ICBMs capable of reaching American territory, heightening American anxiety and demoralization. This sentiment worsened following two unsuccessful attempts by the US Navy's Project Vanguard to launch a smaller American satellite.

While it's well-known that the United States eventually entered orbit with Explorer 1 and ultimately led the space race with the Apollo 11 moon landing, many are unaware of the variety of unusual strategies considered by the US government and military to boost public morale in the interim. One such project was Project A119, initiated in May 1958 by the Armor Research Foundation (ARF) at the Illinois Institute of Technology, under the leadership of the US Air Force. The ARF, having studied nuclear explosions since 1949, adapted its research to explore the effects of such explosions on the lunar surface. This initiative was partly fueled by rumors in American newspapers about a Soviet plan to detonate a nuclear bomb on the moon to mark the 50th anniversary of the October Revolution, coinciding with a lunar eclipse on November 7, 1957. Although such a plan was indeed considered by the Soviet Union, documented evidence of the plan dates only from 1958. No explosion occurred on November 7, but the US government believed that demonstrating the capability to detonate their own lunar explosion could showcase technological superiority and elevate public morale.

At the Illinois Institute of Technology, ARF's team was led by Leonard Rifle, who was confident that the U.S. Air Force's rapid development of ICBMs would make Project A119 feasible by 1959. Rifle believed that with certain technical adjustments, they could achieve an accuracy of hitting a target on the moon's surface within two miles. Initially, the team considered detonating a full hydrogen bomb, but this was deemed impractical by the Air Force due to the excessive payload weight. Instead, they opted for a W-25 warhead, a smaller device relying solely on nuclear fission, not fusion like a hydrogen bomb. Weighing 220 pounds (100 kilograms), the W-25 had a yield of 1.7 kilotons, significantly less than the atomic bombs previously used in warfare and nuclear tests.

To ensure visibility, ARF planned to detonate the warhead along the moon's terminator, the twilight zone between the lunar day and night. This location would enhance the explosion's visibility against the dark backdrop and allow sunlight to illuminate the resulting dust cloud. While the idea of a lunar explosion might seem straightforward, the team had several reservations. Firstly, there was concern that such an explosion could interfere with future scientific studies, such as measuring the moon's natural background radiation. Additionally, with plans for manned lunar missions and poten-tial colonization, there was apprehension about the safety of future lunar explorers due to potential fallout.

Another major worry was the accuracy of the launch. By 1958, no man-made object had reached the moon, and there was a real risk that the missile could miss the moon entirely, potentially re-entering Earth's atmosphere or failing to exit it, which would pose significant risks if debris fell back to a populated area.

Ultimately, these concerns, combined with international treaties like the Partial Nuclear Test Ban Treaty of 1963 and the Outer Space Treaty of 1967, led to the abandonment of Project A119, much like the Soviet Union's analogous project, E4. The exact cancellation date of Project A119 remains unclear due to sparse documentation and public release of related facts.

The public remained completely unaware of Project A119 until 1999 when author Keay Davidson unearthed two scientific papers that hinted at its existence. These papers, titled "Possible Contribution of Lunar Nuclear Weapons Detonations to the Solution of Some Problems in Planetary Astronomy" and "Radiological Contamination of the Moon by Nuclear Weapons Detonations," surfaced in a 1959 scholarship application for the Miller Institute at the University of California, Berkeley. The applicant was the renowned astronomer and science educator Carl Sagan, who had passed away in 1996. In his application, Sagan detailed his involvement with Project A119 during his doctoral studies under advisor Gerhard Kuiper, focusing particularly on the potential visibility of the nuclear explosion's dust cloud, a key element in boosting American morale.

Davidson included these findings in his biography "Carl Sagan: A Life," which was subsequently reviewed in "Nature" magazine. The review discussed Sagan's contribution to the project and raised questions about whether his disclosure in the scholarship application might have constituted a breach of national security and project confidentiality.

Following the publication and growing media interest, Leonard Rifle, the head of the ARF team at the Illinois Institute of Technology, came forward to confirm the project's existence. He revealed that the team was aware of Sagan's disclosure at the time and considered it a breach of confidentiality, although no action was taken against Sagan. This revelation sparked significant public interest and led to a request under the Freedom of Information Act for more details about the project. In response, the Illinois Institute of Technology released "A Study of Lunar Research Flights, Vol. 1," credited to Rifle, but noted that most other documents had been destroyed in the 1980s. To this day, the U.S. government has not officially acknowledged the existence of Project A119.

When Leonard Rifle disclosed the details of Project A119, he did not mince words. At 73, he expressed his dismay that such a plan to influence public opinion was even contemplated. Rifle had attempted to convince the Air Force officials who hired him of the significant scientific costs of damaging the untouched lunar environment. He worried that the explosion would mar the iconic "Man in the Moon" and potentially trigger a militarization of space, escalating into a race for military rather than scientific supremacy if paired with the Soviet's project E4.

With the project's details now public, though unofficially, several figures and academics voiced their disapproval. David Lowry, a British environmental consultant and anti-nuclear activist, described the project as "obscene," lamenting the idea that humanity's first interaction with another celestial body could have been a nuclear explosion. He argued that had the project proceeded, the historic moment of Neil Armstrong's moonwalk would have lacked its profound significance.

However, Lowry also speculated that the desire to militarize space persists, suggesting that what might seem as outlandish as lunar nuclear explosions in the '50s could appear equally incredible today. He hinted at ongoing but unspecified plans that might consider using nuclear detonations for scientific purposes as part of lunar exploration and colonization.

Interestingly, nuclear explosions could still have scientific utility. For example, Edward Teller, known for his role in developing the hydrogen bomb, proposed studies in 1957 that could leverage small-scale nuclear detonations on the moon to analyze its geological structure and the impact of nuclear blasts and radiation on its surface. These insights could help in establishing manned lunar bases, potentially powered by nuclear reactors as envisaged in NASA's Artemis program.

Thus, despite the controversial nature of Project A119, the research associated with it and the involvement of scientists like Carl Sagan and Leonard Rifle might not be entirely fruitless. The first nuclear explosion on the moon might not come from an Earth-launched rocket but could be initiated by explorers on the lunar surface, marking a profound, albeit daunting, milestone in space exploration.

The Exploding Whale of 1970

Why would anyone detonate a whale? In 1970, the quiet town of Florence, Oregon, became the scene of one of the most unusual events ever documented—the infamous exploding whale incident. On November 9th, a massive, deceased sperm whale was discovered on Florence Beach, not far from the south jetty. Weighing eight tons and measuring 45 feet long, it was as big as a typical school bus. The giant carcass, decaying under the sun for several days, began emitting a foul odor that signaled a need for immediate action.

The Oregon Department of Transportation, responsible for managing the state's beaches at the time, was tasked with devising a solution for the removal of the colossal carcass. Whale beachings were rare on the Oregon coast, and no one recalled how a similar incident in 1910 was handled. Options were limited: burying the whale risked it being uncovered by ocean tides, while dismembering it posed logistical nightmares and required volunteers and special equipment. Letting it decompose naturally was too slow and posed health risks due to the enduring stench.

Faced with these challenges, a bold decision was made to eradicate the decaying behemoth by blowing it to smithereens. This decision would lead to a spectacularly misguided outcome. As the putrid smell spread, a crowd of curious onlookers and news crews gathered, including reporter Paul Linnman, who anticipated a light story but ended up witnessing much more. The Oregon State Highway Division, tasked with handling the situation, was confronted with not just a problem, but a stinking whale of a problem. The engineer in charge, George Thornton, advised that dynamite had solved many issues before and was optimistic about its effectiveness, though the exact amount needed was uncertain.

After consultations with the U.S. Navy and munitions experts, it was decided to proceed with the plan. Half a ton of explosives was used, with experts carefully positioning twenty 50-pound cases of dynamite around the whale. As tension mounted, the crowd was moved back to a safe distance, awaiting the impending blast.

Thornton's approach was to treat the whale much like a boulder and blast its remains toward the ocean, where the tide could help in its cleanup. He reassured skeptics that the explosion would reduce the carcass to small, manageable pieces for scavengers to consume. Meanwhile, a passerby with expertise in explosives happened upon the scene in his recently purchased Oldsmobile. He cautioned the highway division that their plan required either less explosives to gently push the whale towards the sea or significantly more to completely disintegrate it. Despite his advice, the planned detonation went ahead.

What ensued was absolute chaos. The explosion sent the whale's massive right side soaring 150 feet into the air, and a mix of whale tissue and sand shot skyward like an erupting volcano. Spectators on the nearby dunes were initially in awe, but humor quickly turned to panic as large chunks of whale flesh flew perilously close. The crowd screamed and scrambled for safety as huge pieces of flesh landed around them. When the news crew realized they were too close, they too fled. As whale remains thudded to the ground, a stark realization hit: the situation was life-threatening.

The most notable casualty of this pandemonium was a car parked 450 feet from the explosion site, which was crushed under a massive chunk of whale the size of a coffee table. Ironically, this was the same Oldsmobile belonging to the man who had warned the officials. He could only watch in dismay as his new car was demolished. It was an ironic twist, especially since he had just bought the car at a dealership promoting it as "a whale of a deal." Within two days, the state of Oregon compensated him for the full retail value of his car.

Amazingly, no one was injured. In the aftermath, Thornton surveyed the site, which was littered with whale parts and scattered blubber. News reporter Linnman described the scene vividly, noting that the explosion sent blubber flying far and wide, creating a massive hole in the beach. A significant portion of the whale still had to be moved and was eventually buried with the assistance of a bulldozer. Smaller pieces of blubber were either discarded or buried in sand. The seagulls, initially expected to feast on the whale remains, were deterred by the explosion and stayed away from the area for a long time.

In the mid-1990s, when contacted by Linnman, Thornton declined an on-camera interview, believing that media coverage had unfairly portrayed a successful operation as a disaster. He tersely suggested that, in his view, nothing had gone wrong. For Linnman, the segment he hesitated to produce became a historical phenomenon, watched over 350 million times across various platforms by 2006.

The tale of the exploding whale served as a cautionary tale; when 41 sperm whales beached themselves in 1979 near Florence, authorities opted to burn and bury the carcasses instead of using explosives. In a display of collective humor, Florence residents later named their latest recreational area Exploding Whale Memorial Park, commemorating the infamous event over 50 years ago. The exploding whale not only left a mess on the beach but also made for a whale of a tale.

Franz Reichelt

On February 4, 1912, Franz Reichelt arrived at the base of the Eiffel Tower, accompanied by a few close friends and a new invention to test—a parachute suit. He planned to demonstrate its effectiveness by dropping a mannequin from the lower deck of the renowned Parisian landmark. Despite his confidence, the test would reveal a critical flaw in his design.

Born on October 16, 1878, in what is now the town of Štětí in the Czech Republic, Reichelt moved to Paris around the age of 20, establishing himself as a skilled tailor. His interest in parachute design sparked in 1910, a time when aviation was still in its infancy. Although people had been flying in balloons for over a century and unpowered gliders were somewhat common, powered, piloted airplanes had only made their debut with the Wright brothers' flight in December 1903.

The era was ripe with innovation, but aviation accidents were not uncommon, fueling a strong interest in developing reliable parachutes for pilots in distress. Previous parachute designs were bulky and not suitable for emergencies. Convinced he could improve on these designs, Reichelt began experimenting with sleek, wearable silk parachutes that could be deployed without hindering the wearer's movement.

His work gained potential momentum when a French colonel offered a prize of 10,000 francs (nearly fifty thousand dollars today) for a viable emergency parachute. Reichelt spent years refining his design and even approached the Aero Club of France for support, though they were skeptical and advised against further development.

Undeterred, Reichelt continued testing with mannequins, most of which were unsuccessful. He described his design as an all-silk garment with a wide hood that would transform into a large umbrella upon deployment. Reichelt himself tested the parachute, jumping from heights of about 10 meters (33 feet), cushioned by straw bales. Despite one jump resulting in a broken leg, he remained convinced of his design's efficacy, believing only greater height was needed for proper deployment.

This determination led him to the Eiffel Tower, seeking a higher vantage point to prove his parachute suit could save aviators during emergencies.

Standing 330 meters (1083 feet) tall, the Eiffel Tower presented a unique challenge for Franz Reichelt. The very top was impractical for a jump due to its design, but Reichelt identified the lowest deck as an ideal location. At a height of 57 meters (187 feet), it offered sufficient time for his parachute to deploy.

Other inventors had been granted permission to conduct tests from this lower deck using mannequins. Initially, Reichelt's requests for similar permission were denied, but after persisting for over a year, the Parisian prefect of police relented. The prefect later clarified that his approval was strictly for tests using mannequins, not for a human jump. Nonetheless, on February 4, 1912, Reichelt arrived at the tower donned in his parachute suit, determined to test it himself. He declared his intention to the gathered journalists, friends, and spectators, stating, "I want to try the experiment myself and without trickery, as I intend to prove the worth of my invention."

Despite attempts by his friends to dissuade him, saying, "You are going to see how my 72 kilos and my parachute will give the most decisive of denials to your arguments," no one could sway him. Reichelt proudly demonstrated the compactness of his suit, which was no bulkier than a standard aviator's outfit, and ascended the tower's 347 steps to the lower deck, accompanied by a cameraman and friends. Another cameraman awaited below to capture his descent.

Once on the first deck, Reichelt prepared by placing a chair on a table to reach the guardrail and tossed a piece of paper to gauge the wind. Despite the cold, breezy conditions, he proceeded. At approximately 8:22 am, after a brief contemplation, he jumped. Tragically, the parachute failed, and he fell to his death. An autopsy later revealed that he not only succumbed to the impact but also suffered a heart attack during the descent.

The aftermath of Reichelt's fatal experiment led to widespread media coverage, often portraying him as either a mad genius or simply mad. His death prompted tighter restrictions on parachute testing from the Eiffel Tower, and permission was generally denied even for tests involving mannequins.

Despite this setback in France, parachute experimentation continued across Europe and America. Although early parachutes were too bulky for practical use during World War I, some observers in balloons managed to escape using parachutes tethered to their balloons. After the war, efforts to develop a compact, wearable parachute intensified. By 1919, the airplane parachute type A was developed, leading to the widespread use of parachutes in World War II and beyond for military, leisure, and emergency purposes.

Franz Reichelt dreamed of revolutionizing aviation with his invention. While history may view him as reckless, his tragic failure was part of the journey towards a technology that has since saved countless lives.

Houdini's Death

When Harry Houdini and his team reached The Garrick Theatre in Detroit, Michigan on October 24, 1926, the renowned Hungarian-born magician and escape artist was suffering from a high fever, ranging between 102 and 104 degrees Fahrenheit. Just two days prior, while resting in his dressing room in Montreal before a performance, a college student named J. Gordon Whitehead approached him. The details of what happened next vary among eyewitnesses. The prevailing account indicates that Whitehead inquired whether Houdini could indeed withstand any blow to his abdomen, as rumored. Houdini affirmed the claim and permitted Whitehead to test it.

While Houdini was still reclining—his mobility compromised due to a broken ankle sustained during his famed Water-Torture Cell escape—Whitehead delivered several punches to Houdini's abdomen. Caught off-guard and unable to brace himself, Houdini endured more pain than expected from the punches and soon signaled Whitehead to stop. Despite the significant pain and his injured ankle, Houdini resolved that the night's show must proceed.

As Houdini headed for his next performance in Detroit, his health significantly worsened. He was feverish and, although he declined hospitalization, he was examined by a doctor before the show who diagnosed him with acute appendicitis and urged immediate surgery. Defiant, Houdini chose to perform, starting with a series of vanishing acts and climaxing by making a woman disappear and replacing her with a flowering shrub. He completed the first act but deteriorated further, requiring his assistant to complete the remainder of the performance.

Post-show, back at his hotel, Houdini's condition did not improve. His wife, Bess, vehemently insisted he receive hospital care, prompting another doctor's visit. This second consultation confirmed the urgent need for hospitalization and surgery. Although initially resistant, Houdini, after discussing with his personal physician, Dr. William Stone, consented and was admitted to Grace Hospital in Detroit for an emergency appendectomy.

Upon his arrival at the hospital, it was confirmed that Harry Houdini was suffering from peritonitis caused by a ruptured appendix. At the time, there was speculation that the punches he received to his abdomen might have triggered his appendicitis. Indeed, the life insurance company concluded that these blows had caused the rupture, resulting in a payout of double indemnity.

While such a diagnosis seemed plausible then, modern medical opinion suggests it's unlikely that the punches directly caused the rupture, as such instances are exceptionally rare. It is believed that Houdini was already experiencing early symptoms of appendicitis at the time he was punched. The additional pain from the blows may have obscured the severity of his condition, leading Houdini to misinterpret the life-threatening appendicitis pain as less serious.

In an era devoid of antibiotics, any secondary infection from a ruptured appendix was typically fatal, making timely surgical intervention crucial. The prevailing theory suggests that if Houdini had not been subjected to the punches, he might have sought medical help sooner. However, this is speculative, as he consistently ignored medical advice even as his condition became critical.

Emergency surgery was performed to remove Houdini's ruptured appendix, but the damage was extensive. He managed to survive for about a week at

Grace Hospital, passing away on October 31, 1926, at the age of 52.

Despite his staunch skepticism of spiritualism, which he actively debunked, Houdini had promised his wife Bess that he would attempt to communicate from beyond if possible, specifically ten years after his death. On Halloween of 1936, Bess held a séance to reach Houdini but was unsuccessful. Since then, many have tried to contact him on Halloween, all without success.

Apart from his legendary magic career, Houdini also dabbled in acting, appearing in several silent films, and was an accomplished pilot. Notably, he made the first successful, sustained, powered flight in Australia. Born Erik Weisz in Budapest, Hungary, on March 24, 1874, he emigrated to the U.S. in 1878 with his family. They settled in Appleton, Wisconsin, where his father worked as a rabbi before moving to Milwaukee after losing his position. Known in his youth as Ehrie, which eventually evolved into Harry, he left school after third grade and ran away from home at the age of 12.

The Tunguska Event of 1908

At 7:17 AM on the 30th of June 1908, a mysterious explosion occurred in the skies above the Tunguska River. Seismic vibrations strong enough to register as the fifth degree on the Richter scale were recorded 1000 km [600 miles] away from the epicenter. At a distance of 500 km [300 miles], witnesses observed loud bangs and a fiery cloud rising above the horizon. Closer, about 170 km [110 mi] from the impact, an object resembling a brilliant, sun-like fireball traveling at high speed was seen in the clear daytime sky, accompanied by thunderous noises. Only 60 km [40 mi] from the center, the force of the explosion knocked people to the ground and shattered windows, sending furniture and other objects tumbling. Near the explosion site, 30 km [20 mi] away, reindeer herders were catapulted through the air by a sudden blast, resulting in injuries and fatalities, including an elderly herder who suffered a fatal compound fracture. The explosion also ignited and toppled trees, which fell in a pattern radiating from the epicenter.

Another herder described the ground shaking and a prolonged roar, surrounded by smoke and fog from burning trees, which eventually quieted down as the forest continued to burn. Many reindeer fled and were lost. In Kirensk and nearby towns, the phenomenon of a fireball slashing across the sky was consistently reported, with observers describing a ball of fire taking a flattened shape as it approached the ground and leaving a trail of varying colors. After the event, distant witnesses saw a vertical column of smoke on the horizon, and in the days following, unusual atmospheric phenomena were reported over Russia and Europe.

The remote location and political instability in Russia at the time delayed further investigation until 1921 when Leonard Kulik, a professor of mineralogy, launched an expedition to explore the area. Initial attempts only identified the general area of the blast, but persistent efforts led to a more comprehensive exploration in 1927 despite challenging conditions and local reluctance due to shamanic beliefs attributing the event to a divine curse. Kulik's team eventually encountered evidence of the devastation firsthand, observing charred trees that had been scorched from above, suggesting an intense heat source rather than a typical forest fire.

Kulik's expedition returned to the dead forest on the 20th of May, finding the trees fallen in a pattern pointing toward what Kulik identified as Ground Zero, located in an area known as the Southern Swamp. As a mineralogist, Kulik initially hypothesized that a meteorite caused the blast. However, upon reaching the epicenter, he discovered no crater and observed a peculiar sight: a forest of charred, branchless trunks standing straight like telephone poles.

The landscape further intrigued Kulik, with the ground appearing to ripple outward in giant waves. With limited supplies, Kulik was compelled to end this trip soon after, though he returned for two additional expeditions in 1929 and 1938, both of which failed to explain the absence of a crater.

In 1940, another scientist, E. L. Krinov, theorized that the meteorite might have exploded mid-air, which could account for the lack of a crater. Yet, no meteoric rock specimens were found, and World War II halted further research, leaving the Tunguska event shrouded in mystery for years.

The late investigation of the event, coupled with the scarcity of information and the secretive nature of the Soviet regimes, fueled a plethora of theories about the nature of the Tunguska blast. Some of these theories are quite outlandish, while others seem more plausible.

One of the more speculative theories came from engineer and sci-fi writer

Aleksander Kasantsews and Soviet scientist Alexei Zolotov, who suggested that a nuclear explosion of extraterrestrial origin was responsible for the Tunguska blast, positing a malfunctioning UFO or an interplanetary weapon as possible causes. Science writer T.R. LeMaire expanded on this, speculating that the object might have been navigated, using Lake Baikal as a reference, and changed direction twice during flight. He also suggested that the timing and clear weather conditions indicated a potentially deliberate act, similar to the historical bombing mission by the Enola Gay, but with a last-minute decision to spare populated areas.

Another theory involves Nikola Tesla and a failed experiment with his Wardenclyffe Tower, which was designed for wireless communication and energy transmission. Some theorize that Tesla might have inadvertently directed a massive energy blast toward the uninhabited North Pole, missing and hitting Tunguska instead. This aligns with claims that the tower could function as a superweapon. Tesla himself later claimed to have designed and tested a beam projector, dubbed Teleforce, which could be seen as a precursor to such technology.

In 1973, a paper published in the journal Nature suggested that a black hole had collided with Earth, causing the Tunguska explosion. This theory, proposed by the Centre for Relativity Theory at the University of Texas, hypothesized that a small black hole descended upon Tunguska, creating the crater-less impact, sped through the Earth, and then exited the planet in the North Atlantic. The theory proposed investigating the ocean floor for an 'exit wound' to validate this hypothesis, but the expedition was never funded, leading to the theory's discreditation. Alongside, another hypothesis within theoretical physics proposed that the Tunguska event could have resulted from a matter and antimatter collision, which would annihilate upon contact, releasing intense bursts of energy, yet this theory also remained unproven.

Further theories emerged following Kulik's expedition, attempting to explain the lack of craters and alien rock fragments at Ground Zero. One such theory suggested that the Tunguska event was caused by an icy fragment of a comet, which would have violently evaporated as it entered Earth's atmosphere, causing the blast. Conversely, a theory in the 1960s proposed a magmatic explanation, speculating that volcanic gases trapped beneath Siberia might have caused the explosions described by witnesses. However, geologists found no evidence of shattered rocks or gas vents to support this.

In 2013, a team led by Victor Kvasnytsya of the National Academy of Sciences of Ukraine analyzed microscopic rock samples from the 1978 site and confirmed they were of meteoric origin, dating back to 1908. The findings suggested that the meteoric fragments were present but had been overlooked due to their small size. These fragments contained lonsdaleite, a mineral formed from meteoric impacts, leading researchers to conclude that the Tunguska event was a natural phenomenon involving a meteor explosion.

These findings contribute to the scientific consensus that the Tunguska event was caused by a large meteor colliding with Earth's atmosphere at about 15 km per second. The atmosphere acted as a shield, vaporizing the meteor into tiny fragments while converting the kinetic energy into heat, explaining the absence of a crater and the extensive damage observed. The intense heat released accounted for the observed blast, shock wave, and forest fires. This event underscores the significant destructive potential of celestial objects and the importance of ongoing research and preparedness for future impacts.

Christmas Banned

In 1659, the General Court of Massachusetts declared it illegal to celebrate Christmas. Anyone caught hosting a feast or even taking the day off on December 25th faced a fine of five shillings. To understand why this law came into effect, it's essential to explore the history of Christmas in the New England colonies during the 1600s. This region was inhabited by Puritan Pilgrims who had been expelled from Anglican England due to their dissenting religious views. These Pilgrims crossed the Atlantic to establish a society that eschewed most of the ceremonies and holidays celebrated by the English, including Christmas.

Like many today who believe Christmas can overshadow its true significance, the Puritans took an even more stringent stance, opposing the celebration of Jesus's birthday altogether. Even before the 1659 prohibition, festivities were discouraged. Historian Stephen Nissenbaum notes that for the first two centuries of European settlement, most New Englanders did not observe Christmas, as reflected in almanacs that meticulously recorded daily details but conspicuously ignored December 25th.

The Puritans argued that the Bible did not mandate the celebration of Christ's birthday and contended that the holiday was rooted in paganism. They pointed out that the choice of December 25th was likely influenced by its proximity to Roman pagan festivals, although historians debate this timing. Early Christians had various reasons for choosing this date, with some, like St. Augustine, suggesting that Christ's birth on the winter solstice symbolized increasing light after the darkest day.

However, a significant reason for Puritan opposition to Christmas was its association with unruly behavior dating back to the Middle Ages. The holiday was linked with excessive drinking, public riots, and social norm reversals. Even pro-Christmas Anglicans like Bishop Hugh Latimer criticized the period for encouraging sinful behaviors, noting that people dishonored Christ more during the Christmas season than throughout the rest of the year.

One particularly contentious tradition was "mumming," where men and women swapped clothes and visited neighbors, often accompanied by demands for food and drink, sometimes under threats of violence. This type of role reversal extended to the tradition of Christmas caroling, where the poor would not serve the wealthy but instead demand hospitality, illustrated by the aggressive tone in the demand for figgy pudding in the carol "We Wish You a Merry Christmas."

Puritans saw no need to exacerbate the already rowdy post-harvest festivities of December and January with Christmas celebrations. Despite this, attitudes began to shift, and in 1681, the Massachusetts Bay Colony's ban was lifted due to pressure from the British crown. Over time, British Christmas sermons and songs gained popularity in Boston, and by the late 1700s, most of colonial society recognized Christmas as a sacred day, although some Calvinists maintained their disdain for the holiday.

Post-independence, various Christian denominations advocated for the recognition of Christmas as a public holiday. The commercialization of Christmas also played a role in shaping the contemporary celebration of the holiday. American retailers promoted toys and other goods, and cultural works like the 1822 poem "'Twas the Night Before Christmas" helped craft the modern image of Santa Claus. Coupled with societal shifts from agriculture to industry, these influences transformed Christmas into a day focused less on boisterous celebration and more on quiet family gatherings.

New England Dark Day of 1780

On May 19, 1917, eighty New Englanders woke up to an eerie, shadowy fog obscuring the morning sun. By midday, the sky was as dark as midnight, confusing even the local wildlife; night birds sang and chickens roosted prematurely. People resorted to lighting candles to see in the unexpected darkness. It took scientists two centuries to identify the likely cause of this mysterious event. At the time, many Americans feared it signaled the biblical end times. This event has since been commemorated as the Dark Day of 1780.

In the days leading up to May 19, 1917, unusual phenomena were noted in the skies. Following one of the coldest winters on record, the still, breezy air warmed but remained unusually dense. During dusk and dawn, the sun appeared reddish, and the moon glowed pink in the evenings. Even General George Washington, stationed in New Jersey, recorded in his diary "heavy and uncommon kinds of clouds" and a strange intermix of darkness and reddish light.

The morning of May 19 started gloomy and calm, with a light drizzle in some areas. As residents of New Hampshire, Maine, Massachusetts, Rhode Island, and Connecticut began their day, they noticed an ominous change between 8:00 and 9:00 AM. Reddish-orange clouds rolled in from the west, dimming the sun further and casting the skies in shades of apple cider. By noon, the sun was completely obscured, plunging most of New England into darkness, prompting people to light candles to continue their daily activities.

Many people resorted to working by candlelight, while others could only pause and marvel at the extraordinary events unfolding around them, mistaking the early darkness for nightfall. Owls hooted, crickets chirped, and even the flowers closed their petals as if night had fallen. On this day, during a session of the Governor's Council of Connecticut, some politicians, unnerved by the darkness, suggested adjourning the meeting. However, Councilman Abraham Davenport, a militia colonel from Connecticut, staunchly opposed this. He famously declared, "The day of judgment is either approaching or it is not. If it is not, there is no cause for adjournment; if it is, I choose to be found doing my duty. I wish therefore that candles may be brought." Inspired by his resolve, the council agreed to continue their session by candlelight.

This courageous stance by Davenport later became legendary, immortalized in an 1866 poem by John Greenleaf Whittier. Throughout the day, a few rays of sunlight managed to pierce the pervasive darkness, but the eerie gloom largely persisted, leading to what many described as one of the darkest nights recorded, disrupting sleep as people feared they might never see daylight again.

With little scientific understanding prevalent among New England's 1780 population, the sudden darkness caused considerable alarm, leading many to turn to their religious beliefs for comfort. In a predominantly Protestant society, natural phenomena were often seen as signs or divine messages, with some interpreting the event as fulfilling biblical prophecies from the Book of Revelation about the sun turning black and the moon blood red.

The lack of immediate communication compounded the fear and confusion. Without cellphones or rapid means to disseminate information, people were largely unaware of what was happening beyond their immediate surround-ings, relying on word of mouth in a time when neighbors were often miles apart. The unexpected darkness challenged their fundamental reliance on the predictable cycle of day and night.

Decades and even centuries later, several theories were proposed to explain the Dark Day of 1780, including a massive cloud cover, a solar eclipse, a volcanic eruption, and a meteor strike. However, none of these explanations proved satisfactory; a thick cloud or solar eclipse, for instance, would not account for such prolonged darkness, and there was no evidence of volcanic activity or a meteor strike at that time. Thus, the mystery of New England's Dark Day remained largely unexplained, a curious historical anomaly.

However, science finally resolved this longstanding mystery in 2008. Researchers at the University of Missouri uncovered what they believe to be the most plausible cause of the sudden darkness in New England on May 19, 1780. Their study, "Fire-Scarred Trees Reveal Source of New England's 1780 Dark Day," published in the International Journal of Wildland Fire, presented evidence from tree rings in Ontario, Canada. These rings indicated that a massive wildfire in 1780 likely sent columns of dense smoke high into the upper atmosphere, significantly impacting the atmospheric conditions hundreds of miles away.

This finding was supported by various historical accounts. For instance, Boston geographer Jeremy Belknap wrote in a letter to Ebenezer Hazard in 1780, describing the air as smelling like a malt house or a coal kiln, suggesting the presence of ash. Observations from the time also noted that bodies of water appeared unusually murky and dark.

The University of Missouri's study bridged historical narratives with modern scientific techniques through the analysis of tree rings. This integration led to a comprehensive explanation of an event that had puzzled observers for centuries. While the people of New England in 1780, lacking concrete evidence, continued to view the Dark Day with a mix of fear and awe, the scientific explanation provided by this study offers a clear, rational understanding of the events. This mysterious day has since been woven into the region's cultural fabric, remembered through various artistic and poetic interpretations.

Tsutomu Yamaguchi

Tsutomu Yamaguchi, the man who survived two atomic bombings, epitomizes being in the wrong place at the wrong time more than anyone else. As the first officially recognized survivor of both the Hiroshima and Nagasaki bombings, Yamaguchi's story is a remarkable account of survival against all odds. It was the morning of August 6, 1945, just one month shy of World War II's conclusion. Having completed a three-month stint at Mitsubishi Heavy Industries in Hiroshima, where he designed oil tankers, Yamaguchi was preparing to return home to Nagasaki to reunite with his wife and newborn son. The 29-year-old realized he had forgotten his hanko, a common identification stamp in Japan, and decided to retrieve it. As he was heading back, he heard a rumbling overhead and saw an American B-29 bomber release a small object attached to parachutes. Moments later, a blinding white light engulfed him, and he managed to dive into a ditch just before a sonic boom resonated, plunging everything into darkness.

Upon waking, Yamaguchi found himself amidst debris, barely able to see the sun through the dust and smoke. Despite severe injuries and burst eardrums, he was miraculously alive, less than two miles from ground zero. The city had suffered greatly, with approximately 30% of its population perishing instantly, and many more dying in the following months.

Years later, in a British interview, Yamaguchi described the horrific scene: a towering mushroom cloud rising, prismatic lights shifting like a kaleidoscope. His first instinct was to ensure he could still move his legs. Knowing he had to leave to survive, he made his way back to the shipyard. Miraculously, he discovered that two colleagues had also survived. Together, they spent a day and night in an air raid shelter before making their way to a functioning railway station, navigating through a landscape littered with corpses and destruction.

Meanwhile, President Truman in America had boldly claimed responsibility for the atomic bomb, warning Japan of further devastation if they did not surrender. Amidst these dire circumstances and still severely injured, Yamaguchi returned to work on August 9, only to be reprimanded by his boss, who disbelieved a single bomb could have caused such destruction and accused Yamaguchi of madness. As they argued, another blinding flash of light—the onset of the Nagasaki bombing—filled the office, marking the second atomic explosion Yamaguchi would miraculously survive.

At 11:02 AM on August 9th, the second atomic bomb was dropped on Nagasaki, adding seventy thousand more victims to the tragic toll. Tsutomu Yamaguchi, still reeling from injuries and his recent ordeal in Hiroshima, momentarily believed the mushroom cloud had chased him to Nagasaki. Overcome with frustration and ignoring the pleas of his injured boss, Yamaguchi escaped through a shattered window and rushed to his family. Fortunately, his wife and baby were safe, with only minor injuries. Exhausted and severely wounded, Yamaguchi spent the following week teetering on the brink of life and death, battling fever and painful burns in a city where medical facilities had been obliterated.

A week later, amidst his struggle for survival, Japan announced its surrender on August 15, 1945. The decision to use atomic bombs continues to spark debate over their morality and necessity. The hastened surrender of Japan poses the question: Did it justify the massive loss of life, or were the bombings unnecessary atrocities that amounted to war crimes? Notably, the U.S. had additional atomic bombs prepared, pending President Truman's approval just days before Japan's capitulation. Had these bombs been used, perceptions of the U.S. role in the war might differ starkly today.

The lingering effects of the bombings and their radiation continue to impact the health of survivors' descendants. Yamaguchi's son tragically died at 59 from cancer caused by radiation exposure as an infant. Many others have suffered similar fates. Yamaguchi himself survived his son, enduring deafness in one ear and other chronic health issues, while his wife succumbed to radiation-induced organ failure at 88. Despite these hardships, Yamaguchi lived to be 93, passing away in 2010 from stomach cancer.

Survivors, known as hibakusha, receive government support and healthcare. Initially recognized only as a survivor of the Nagasaki bombing, Yamaguchi later sought dual recognition to share the harrowing experiences of the atomic bombings with future generations. In 2009, he was officially acknowledged as a survivor of both bombings. In his later years, Yamaguchi expressed that the U.S. might have demonstrated their power sufficiently with a single bomb, questioning the necessity of the second.

Hiroo Onoda

In 1945, during World War II, Japanese Second Lieutenant Hiroo Onoda and three other soldiers were the sole survivors of an American assault on Lubang Island in the Philippines. Committed to his directive to defend the island at all costs, Onoda continued his resistance against Allied forces until 1974—29 years after Japan had surrendered.

Surviving off the wilderness and engaging in guerrilla warfare against locals, Onoda persisted in his combat efforts for three decades post-war. In today's episode of Weird History, we'll explore the story of Hiroo Onoda, the man who continued fighting World War II 30 years after its conclusion.

Initially trained as an intelligence officer and commando, Onoda was tasked with destroying key targets on Lubang Island to hinder American forces. However, a last-minute change in orders left these targets intact, enabling the Americans to capture Lubang in 1945. The idea of openly criticizing his superiors must have been tempting for Onoda as he watched the invasion unfold.

As the Pacific War intensified, casualties mounted, leaving Onoda and his three comrades as the last Japanese military presence on the island. Rising to the highest rank by default, Onoda led his men into the mountains, operating under orders to never surrender or take their own lives. They continued their guerrilla operations with the aim of resisting the American and Filipino forces.

Despite Japan's surrender in September 1945, Onoda and his squad dismissed reports of the war's end as enemy propaganda, choosing instead to remain concealed. This skepticism wasn't unique to Onoda; many Japanese soldiers stranded across the Pacific similarly refused to believe the war had concluded.

Onoda's dedication to the fight paralleled someone who might play Monopoly until the bitter end. Over time, however, his men dwindled: Private Akatsu surrendered in 1950, Corporal Shimada was killed by a search patrol in 1954, and Private First Class Kozuka died during a sabotage mission in 1972. Remarkably, Onoda's stint in the wilderness, waging a nonexistent war, lasted longer than the Beatles' entire career.

Hiroo Onoda emerged as a kind of specter from the jungle, attacking farmers and police like a stealthy predator for decades. He shockingly beheaded a farmer, rationalizing his brutal actions as mere wartime strategies necessary for the conflict he mistakenly thought was ongoing. Onoda described his actions as appearing suddenly to destroy and intimidate, and even set fires in unoccupied houses.

With scant supplies, Onoda and his team retreated into the jungle, continuing World War II for an additional 30 years. As expert survivalists, they subsisted on wild fruits and vegetables, occasionally supplemented by cattle pilfered from local farms. They constructed bamboo shelters and meticulously maintained their gear, ever ready for an inspection by a superior officer. They steadfastly dismissed any news about the war's conclusion or the advancements of the modern world, to the extent that they likely deemed the moon landing a fabrication.

Declared dead by Japan in 1959, Onoda's existence became a myth after the death of PFC Kozuka in 1972 prompted a reevaluation. The media speculated about his survival, turning him into an urban legend. In 1974, Norio Suzuki embarked on a quest to locate Onoda, a panda, and the Abominable Snowman, in that order. Suzuki found Onoda and convinced him to consider that the war might indeed be over. Onoda promised not to harm Suzuki but insisted on remaining until he received direct orders from his commanding officer.

Suzuki returned to Japan, miraculously located Onoda's former commander, Major Taniguchi, now a bookstore clerk. Alongside Suzuki and Onoda's brother, Taniguchi traveled to Lubang Island to formally relieve Onoda of his duties. Initially skeptical, Onoda awaited a covert signal that never came; he fainted upon realizing the legitimacy of Taniguchi's commands and the war's end 29 years prior.

Onoda's surrender was delicate, given his long history of violence in the Philippines, where he had killed at least seven locals. Yet, the Philippine president pardoned him, admiring his resolve and endurance. Onoda, in his long-preserved uniform, presented his sword to the president, who returned it in a gesture of respect.

Returning to Japan, Onoda received a hero's welcome. The media celebrated his unwavering dedication, portraying him as a symbol of national pride during a time of increasing materialism. He authored "No Surrender," a memoir that became essential reading for its portrayal of resilience.

Finding modern Japan bewildering after three decades of isolation, Onoda moved to Brazil with his brother to farm cattle, marrying a woman who shared his traditional values. Disturbed by a tragic incident in Japan, he returned to establish a youth camp to foster resilience and confidence in young people. Onoda also lectured about his beliefs that nature could help find one's purpose.

Despite a full military pension and book royalties, Onoda declined 29 years of back pay and private donations, contributing instead to a Shinto shrine. He passed away in 2014, a steadfast soldier who lived by his duty until the very end, recognizing the conclusion of World War II only upon his commander's confirmation.

Tulip Mania

In the 17th century, Amsterdam flourished as an international port, significantly boosted by the spice trade. This prosperity attracted wealthy merchants, akin to spice traders seeking quick profits. Indeed, there's truth in the sayings about spice enhancing life and consciousness. However, this narrative concerns a different commodity. The affluent established their roots in Amsterdam, building lavish mansions adorned with flowers, particularly tulips, which were deemed exotic at the time.

Similar to today, the wealthy attributed extraordinary value to these flowers, amassing wealth through them. At one point, tulips were as prized as diamonds, with a single Semper Augustus bulb valued at 150 Florence in 1636—equivalent to about $25,000 today, or ten times the annual earnings of a skilled craftsman. Spending $25,000 on a flower might seem ludicrous, but the situation was even more bizarre. Many never saw the tulips bloom; instead, the bulbs were traded from one owner to another, each hoping to turn a greater profit.

As this frenzy continued, the introduction of multicolored tulips, caused by a virus that affected pigmentation, revolutionized the market. Traders were captivated by these unique hues, unaware that they resulted from the Tulip Breaking Virus. To the wealthy, these were merely intriguing novelties. The craze for these virus-stricken tulips might seem farcical, yet truth can be stranger than fiction.

Tulips became a fad, with prices reaching up to 10,000 Guilders at the peak of the craze—an economic bubble poised to burst. The tulip mania nearly devastated Holland's economy, a startling fact considering tulips aren't native to the region.

Pop culture often reduces Dutch imagery to wooden clogs and windmills, but the Netherlands boasts a rich cultural history that goes far beyond these stereotypes. Central to this heritage are tulips, a symbol strongly associated with Dutch identity. These flowers line the streets of Amsterdam, making them a common sight for anyone walking through the city. Interestingly, tulips, now considered the national flower, did not originate in the Netherlands but likely came from what is now modern Kazakhstan.

Dutch traders initially brought tulip bulbs back from their travels, unaware that these would later play a role in economic upheaval due to a phenomenon known as tulip mania. These bulbs, particularly those affected by a disease that caused striking multicolor patterns, became incredibly valuable. The durability of the bulbs made them ideal for trade, as opposed to the delicate flowers which could have slowed down the trading process.

At the peak of tulip mania, bulbs with distinctive patterns, especially those resembling a candy cane, fetched astronomical prices. These were known as the Switzer pattern, a rare and highly sought-after variety. The craze reached such heights that one merchant reportedly traded his house for just 10 of these bulbs, leading to financial ruin for many when the bubble burst a year later. This event profoundly impacted Dutch moral consciousness, leading to a lasting saying that warns against prioritizing fleeting wealth over honor, similar to the Dutch phrases "honor above goods" or "honor above wealth."

The consequences of tulip mania were severe, not only causing housing crises but also leading to incarcerations as the market collapsed. This period remains a poignant lesson in the dangers of speculative bubbles and the values of prudence and honor.

Some state laws might seem quirky, like mandating that pickles must bounce or prohibiting picnics in cemeteries, but these pale in comparison to an incident during tulip mania. Consider the tale of a hungry sailor who, mistaking a tulip bulb for an onion, added it to his herring sandwich. This mistake cost him dearly when the merchant, who owned the valuable Semper Augustus bulb—worth as much as a small mansion in Amsterdam—had him jailed for a felony.

While this story is likely apocryphal, it highlights the absurdity of the tulip trade, as noted by historian Ann Goldgar in her book "Tulipmania: Money, Honor, and Knowledge in the Dutch Golden Age." The idea that tulips were ever consumed as food is dismissed as preposterous until necessity made them so during World War II. Yet, during the tulip mania, the obsession was not about utility but about rarity and prestige. Dutch botanists, driven by competition, pushed the boundaries of horticulture, creating tulips with unusual color combinations that skyrocketed in value.

This competitive spirit spilled over into the taverns where bulb trading became a high-stakes, alcohol-fueled affair, almost a spectator sport with its own drama and tales of grandeur. What began as a gentlemanly pursuit devolved into barroom brawls and financial despair, all over flowers that many never even saw bloom.

Historians suggest that the bubonic plague, which devastated regions like the Dutch municipality of Haarlem, might have precipitated the mania, as patterns of risky behavior often surface during periods of turmoil. As the plague spread, fear kept people away from tulip auctions, contributing to the market's collapse. Over time, the realization dawned that the high prices didn't make sense, leading to a rapid decline in bulb values and widespread financial damage. The government intervened to mitigate some losses, an early form of a bailout.

Anne Goldgar's research indicates that tulip mania was not as widespread as often portrayed, involving only a small fraction of the population in affected cities. However, its legacy as a cautionary tale persists, reminiscent of other speculative bubbles like the Beanie Babies craze of the 1990s. Just as collectors once hoped for a resurgence in Beanie Baby values, similar patterns of speculative investment have recurred throughout history, demonstrating the dangers of commodities soaring far beyond their intrinsic worth. Tulip mania, often likened to the cryptocurrency frenzy of the 21st century, serves as a perennial reminder of the risks inherent in market exuberance.

Count Saint-Germain

The Count of Saint Germain was a European adventurer who rose to prominence in mid-18th century European high society, acclaimed for his contributions to science, alchemy, philosophy, and the arts. His records begin in 18th century Europe, appearing at various social gatherings and royal courts. His multitude of talents, good looks, and extensive knowledge raised suspicions. Questions about his origins, his extensive knowledge, and his involvement in political circles led some to speculate that he might have been a prince, a spy, or an occult mastermind, possibly possessing the secret to eternal life.

Despite the mysteries surrounding him, Saint Germain was undoubtedly a real figure. Prince Charles of Hesse-Cassel regarded him as one of the greatest philosophers to have lived. His existence was further validated by notable 18th-century figures including writer and politician Horace Walpole, who noted that Saint Germain spoke multiple languages fluently and was arrested on espionage charges in London in 1743, only to be released and expelled from England.

Saint Germain reappeared at the French court of King Louis XV, but after political turmoil, he returned to England. Renowned for his charm and intelligence, his youthful appearance fueled rumors of his immortality. Despite having admirers, he also faced criticism, including from French writer and philosopher Voltaire, who sarcastically commented on Saint Germain's reputed immortality and omniscience. The infamous Giacomo Casanova also described him as an unparalleled conversationalist who captivated his audience without partaking in meals, focusing instead on engaging those around him. Saint Germain's life remains a blend of confirmed facts and intriguing myths, leaving his true story partly shrouded in mystery.

He was a multifaceted man, a scholar, linguist, musician, and chemist, known not only for his good looks but also as a perfect ladies' man. He gained the favor of Madame de Pompadour, the chief mistress of King Louis XV, who introduced him to the king. Impressed by Saint Germain, the king provided him with a suite of rooms at Chambord and a hundred thousand francs to build a laboratory.

Despite his claims, which bordered on the incredible—like asserting he was centuries old, knew the secret of universal medicine, had mastery over nature, and could meld diamonds into larger, flawless ones without losing weight— his charisma was undeniable. Even those who recognized his exaggerations and eccentricities found him astonishing rather than offensive.

Voltaire noted Saint Germain's ability to captivate, particularly the ladies. Lady Jemima, a London noble and socialite, once wrote about his intense charm, suggesting that his presence was overwhelmingly persuasive.

Saint Germain was indeed a great storyteller and a man keen on forming powerful connections. However, the allure of his story intensifies with his alleged ties to forbidden knowledge. Rumors circulated that he was an adept alchemist capable of transforming diamonds and producing gold from lead. Further, he was believed to be connected to secretive brotherhoods such as the Illuminati, the Templars, and the Freemasons.

A significant aspect of Saint Germain's mystique was the claim of his extreme age, with some suggesting he could be the legendary Wandering Jew, a figure cursed to live until the Second Coming of Christ. This idea was linked to medieval stories like that of Cartophilus, who purportedly lived since the time of Jesus Christ.

One intriguing incident occurred in Paris in 1760, involving Countess Georgie who attended a soiree at Madame de Pompadour's residence. The Countess, having met Saint Germain in Venice in 1710, was astonished to see he hadn't aged. When she questioned him, he intriguingly claimed to be the same man she knew from Venice, hinting at a near-century of life, which left the Countess astounded at his seemingly perpetual youth.

The Count matter-of-factly convinced the Countess that he was indeed the same man she knew, detailing their previous encounter and life events from 15 years earlier. During his years at the court of Louis XV, Saint Germain was tasked with clandestine operations, including espionage activities in England following a reported dispute with French officials. He is also rumored to have undertaken similar assignments for Germany and to have been involved in a Russian plot to dethrone Tsar Peter III in favor of Catherine the Great. Some even suggest he returned to France to warn Louis XVI and Marie Antoinette of the impending French Revolution, advice that was reportedly unheeded.

Saint Germain's life reportedly ended in 1784 while residing in the home of Prince Charles of Hesse-Cassel in Germany, where he made an astonishing confession on his deathbed. He claimed to be a deposed Transylvanian prince named Francis Rákóczi II, boasting of an exceptional education from the University of Siena. However, historical records indicate that Francis Rákóczi II died in 1735, leading many to suspect Saint Germain was still masking the truth.

Despite his alleged death, sightings of Saint Germain continued. He was reportedly seen with hypnotist Anton Mesmer in Germany in 1785, discussing advanced topics in magnetism. That same year, he was said to have attended a Freemason convention. Following the fall of the Bastille, he supposedly conversed with French nobility about the nation's future, with encounters lasting until 1820 without showing signs of aging.

By the 19th century, suspicions arose that Saint Germain had faked his death and assumed a new identity. Notably, a figure named Major Frazier hinted at historical insights from figures like Nero and Dante. Later, mystic Helena Blavatsky claimed Saint Germain was still active, promoting spiritual awareness and becoming a central figure in Theosophy and other metaphysical disciplines.

Saint Germain's legend took a dark turn with tales of him as a vampire in New Orleans in 1904, where after a series of mysterious parties, he vanished following allegations of trying to drink a woman's blood, leaving behind a house with bloodstains and no sign of food.

The last well-known figure linked to Saint Germain was Richard Chanfrey, a Frenchman in the 1970s who appeared on television claiming to be the Count and demonstrating alchemy. However, Chanfrey's life ended in suicide in 1983, leaving questions about whether this too was part of an ongoing ruse, and if Saint Germain is still out there, living under another guise.

Cottingley Fairies

By the 1910s, scientific curiosity had become a familiar part of everyday life, either practiced seriously or as leisure by people or observed among family members. When the Great War wreaked havoc, leaving deep emotional scars, many sought comfort in the spiritualist and theosophical practices that echoed the scientific investigations of their youth. This return to the enchanting beliefs of childhood, such as fairies, served as a coping mechanism, similar to how some people today might rewatch beloved TV shows from their youth during tough times.

By then, the perception of fairies had shifted significantly. Once considered malevolent spirits, they were now depicted in children's media as benign, playful beings who dwelled in forests and gardens, engaging in small tasks and enjoying harmless fun. Theosophy and spiritualism attempted to rationalize the existence of fairies by likening them to energetic ectoplasm, akin to ghosts or angels, suggesting that they manifest in forms influenced by collective human imagination.

This pseudoscientific theory bridged the gap between the existence of ghosts and fairies, proposing that any proof of one could validate the existence of the other. However, fairy sightings were predominantly reported by children, and in an era before widespread access to cameras, these encounters remained undocumented. It wasn't until 1917 that two young girls from Cottingley, England, borrowed a camera to capture evidence of the fairies they claimed to see, aiming to convince their parents and others of their real experiences with these mystical beings.

Elsie Wright, born in 1901, left school at 13 to work in a Bradford photography studio. Artistic by nature and having attended Bradford College of Art, Elsie found the task of spotting black and white prints stifling to her creativity. After leaving this job and before starting another in photography, the Wright family welcomed Elsie's cousin, Francis Griffiths, and her mother, Annie, who had returned from South Africa where Francis's father was stationed during World War I. The year was 1917, and it marked the beginning of a summer filled with adventures for Elsie and Francis, especially around the Cottingley Beck near the Wrights' home. Francis, often finding herself soaked after playing in the beck, cherished these moments particularly because, despite struggling to make friends at school, she found companionship in what she claimed were fairies.

Francis, decades later, remembered spending afternoons sitting quietly on a willow branch, absorbed in the sounds of nature, when she first saw a small man, about 18 inches tall, manipulating a willow leaf as he crossed the water. This sighting didn't surprise her; the beck was a magical place for her, where anything seemed possible. She kept this secret to herself, not wanting to share these magical encounters.

After being repeatedly questioned by adults about her frequent visits to the beck, a frustrated Francis finally confessed through tears that she went there to see fairies. Elsie also admitted seeing them, but their claims were met with laughter from the adults. Determined to prove their truth, in early July, Elsie borrowed her father Arthur Wright's quarter-plate camera—referred to by some as a Midge—and the girls set out to capture photographic evidence. Within an hour, they returned and excitedly asked Arthur to develop the film. The resulting images, though blurry, showed shapes that resembled fairies, and the girls declared their vindication.

Despite their enthusiasm, Arthur remained skeptical, and two months later, a second photo attempt still didn't convince the parents. While Francis and Elsie were at school, the adults conducted a thorough search of the beck, the glen, and the girls' bedroom for any signs of trickery, like paper cuttings or art scraps, but found nothing. The earnest and casual manner in which the girls spoke of the fairies puzzled the adults, as neither girl was known to lie. Francis even mentioned the fairies nonchalantly in a letter to a friend in South Africa, contrasting her encounters in England with her fairy-less experiences in Africa's heat.

This is where the Theosophical Society and Edward Gardner enter our story. In the summer of 1919, the Bradford Theosophical Society hosted a meeting about fairies, which Annie and Polly, now intrigued by Theosophy since the fairy photographs, attended. During the meeting, Polly mentioned the photographs taken by Frances and Elsie, catching the attention of a friend of Edward Gardner, a prominent figure in the Theosophical movement. Gardner, intrigued, requested to see the photographs. Initially skeptical due to his experience with numerous forgeries, he obtained the original negatives to have them examined by Harold Snelling, an expert in identifying fake photography.

Gardner described the moment Snelling inspected the negatives: he paused, switched on a light under a glass-top desk, and began scrutinizing the images with various lenses. After a lengthy examination, Snelling concluded that the images were genuine single exposures, noting the figures were neither made of paper nor fabric and appeared to have moved during the exposure. Astonished, Gardner realized this might be the first authentic photographic evidence of fairies. He commissioned Snelling to produce high-quality prints and slides, slightly fading Frances's face to highlight the fairies, creating the iconic images known today.

These photographs later caught the attention of Sir Arthur Conan Doyle, famed creator of Sherlock Holmes and a staunch believer in the supernatural, including fairies, ghosts, and angels. His interest was deepened by personal tragedies and the losses he suffered during the war, which reinforced his spiritual beliefs. He was a member of the Society for Psychical Research, a group devoted to investigating paranormal phenomena. Conan Doyle was so committed to his beliefs that he led a mass resignation from the society in the 1920s due to its skepticism, which he found amusingly insufficient.

Conan Doyle's convictions were famously at odds with those of his friend Harry Houdini, who was a skeptic and repeatedly tried to show Doyle that supernatural events could be simulated through trickery. In one instance, Houdini demonstrated a trick involving a hidden message, urging Doyle not to quickly attribute unexplained phenomena to the supernatural. However, Doyle remained unconvinced, even claiming his wife, a medium, could communicate with Houdini's deceased mother, despite a glaring language barrier noted by Houdini.

The friendship eventually deteriorated as Houdini continued to expose fraudulent mediums, contrasting sharply with Doyle's unwavering belief in spiritual powers, which he even attributed to Houdini himself, claiming he was denying his true abilities.

Arthur Conan Doyle did not pass up the chance to dive deeper into the fairy phenomenon when he acquired copies of the Cottingley fairy photos in 1919. This opportunity was timely, as he had been commissioned by The Strand Magazine to pen an article on fairies for their Christmas 1920 issue. Alongside Edward Gardner, a key figure in the Theosophical Society, they set out to meet the Wrights and the Griffiths. By this time, Frances and Elsie were 13 and 19 years old respectively. Gardner, fearing that the girls might marry and move away before they could engage further, hastened the process. They submitted the photos, modified by Snelling, to Kodak for analysis. Although the technicians confirmed the photos were not fabricated, they remained skeptical about their depiction of real fairies, stating that such beings couldn't possibly exist.

Despite this setback, Conan Doyle and Gardner chose to focus on the affirmation that the photos were not recognized as forgeries. Gardner visited Cottingley in July 1920; Frances had already relocated to North Yorkshire with her father, so Gardner spoke with Elsie and explored the glen where the photos were taken. Despite Elsie's casual responses, Gardner remained convinced of the supernatural explanation, believing the girls had psychic abilities.

Eventually, the family consented to have the photos published in The Strand under pseudonyms, with the Wright family renamed the Carpenters and Frances becoming Alice. The issue quickly sold out, drawing a mixed reaction. Some were enchanted, believing it to be proof of fairies, while others, like author Maurice Hewlett, remained skeptical, suggesting that the girls had simply tricked Sir Arthur Conan Doyle.

The story escalated, prompting The Westminster Gazette to dispatch a reporter to unearth more about the girls' backgrounds, though no evidence of deceit was found. Riding the wave of public fascination, Conan Doyle published "The Coming of the Fairies" in 1922, which, despite dwindling interest, sold well initially.

As years passed, interest in the Cottingley fairies waned, and Elsie and Frances moved on to start new lives away from the public eye. It wasn't until 1965 that the story resurfaced when Elsie was interviewed by a Daily Express reporter, maintaining her stance amid skepticism.

By the late 1970s, technological advancements led to a renewed scrutiny of the photos. James "The Amazing" Randi, a magician and paranormal photo debunker, analyzed the images, asserting they were merely cardboard cutouts. Around the same time, Professor Joe Cooper became deeply involved with the story, forming a bond with Frances, who eventually confessed to him in 1981 at Canterbury Cathedral that the photos were staged. This revelation shattered many, including Cooper, who had invested belief in their authenticity.

The tale of the Cottingley fairies, initially a harmless prank by two young girls, spiraled beyond their control, spurred by a public eager to believe in the magical. Even after the truth was revealed, many continued to hold onto their belief in fairies. This story, emblematic of the power of belief and the media's role in shaping perceptions, persists as a fascinating chapter in the intersection of folklore and early 20th-century spiritualism.

Pig War of 1859

The Pig War of 1859 remains one of Britain's most obscure and peculiar episodes in its extensive and vibrant history. During a tense standoff, over 400 U.S. soldiers faced off against five Royal Navy warships on a small island situated between Vancouver and Seattle. This overlooked incident nearly reignited conflict between the United Kingdom and the United States—all sparked by the killing of a pig. Here is the narrative of the Pig War of 1859.

The origins of this conflict trace back to a minor detail in a treaty inked over a decade earlier. Throughout the early 19th century, both the British and Americans had staked claims to the region stretching from the Rocky Mountains to the Pacific coast, now part of the U.S. states of Oregon and Washington and the Canadian province of British Columbia. The Oregon Treaty of 1846 eventually established the 49th parallel of north latitude as the border from the mountains to the sea, a boundary that persists to this day. The treaty also granted the British full control of Vancouver Island.

However, the treaty left a critical ambiguity. Though Vancouver Island extended south of the 49th parallel, it was unclear where the maritime boundary between the British and the Americans lay. The treaty specified that the border would run through the middle of the channel separating the continent from Vancouver Island. But the waters were complicated by the presence of a small group of islands, creating several potential channels. The Americans claimed that the Haro Strait, between San Juan Island and

Vancouver Island, was the boundary. This was strategically near the British town of Victoria at the southern tip of the main island. Conversely, the British favored the Rosario Strait to the east as the border, which would grant them control of these islands, including the pivotal San Juan Island just seven miles from Victoria.

In 1853, the USA formally claimed San Juan Island, but the British, already with a settlement there, ignored this. The Hudson Bay Company had established a salmon curing station on the island in 1851 and a sheep ranch in 1853, seemingly adhering to the maxim that possession is nine-tenths of the law. By 1856, ten years post-treaty, the two nations formed a boundary commission to resolve this dispute but failed to reach a consensus. The British highlighted their commercial interests and settlements on the island, prompting 29 American settlers to swiftly move there.

Although San Juan Island was modest in size, it comfortably accommodated both British and American settlers, who initially coexisted peacefully. However, everything changed on June 15, 1859, transforming this diplomatic impasse into the brink of war over a deceased pig.

American settler Lyman Cutler peered out his window to see a pig uprooting his potato patch. The pig, owned by Hudson Bay Company employee Charles Griffin, was one of several that roamed freely on the island, often causing trouble in Cutler's garden. Frustrated, Cutler grabbed his rifle and shot the pig.

When Griffin discovered what had happened, he confronted Cutler. In the heated exchange that followed, Cutler justified his actions by stating, "I shot the pig because it was eating my potatoes." Griffin retorted, "It's up to you to keep your potatoes out of my pig." In an attempt to resolve the issue, Cutler offered £10 as compensation, but Griffin demanded £100. When Cutler refused, Griffin left in a huff, possibly threatening legal action. He then sought the intervention of the British authorities in nearby Vancouver Island, demanding Cutler's arrest and the expulsion of the American settlers he viewed as trespassers.

The dispute escalated as one of the American settlers, Paul Hobbs, a veteran of the Mexican-American War, contacted an old comrade, Captain George Pickett, who was stationed in Oregon. Pickett's name might ring a bell—he later fought at Gettysburg. Hobbs's plea reached Pickett's superior, Brigadier General William Harney, a seasoned military leader known for his role in the Mexican War and the first Sioux War. Viewing the British claim as a threat to U.S. sovereignty, Harney ordered Pickett and 64 men from the 9th U.S. Infantry to San Juan Island to prevent any British action.

This overreaction to a minor incident was emblematic of the era's tensions. Britain was recovering from the Crimean War and the Sepoy Rebellion, while the U.S. was on the brink of civil war over slavery issues. Intriguingly, some speculated that Harney and Pickett were attempting to provoke a war with Britain to unite the North and South against a common foe. Others suggested it was a distraction engineered by Southern sympathizers to shift Northern focus as Southern states planned secession.

The British responded to the U.S. military presence on San Juan by sending the HMS Tribune, a frigate with 31 guns, from Victoria to confront them. Instead of backing down, Pickett defiantly arranged his men in a battle line on the beach, declaring his readiness to turn it into a "Bunker Hill," referencing the costly Revolutionary War battle where Americans, despite losing, inflicted heavy casualties on the British. Whether Pickett was seeking glory or deliberately provoking a conflict remains a subject for debate.

Fortunately, the captain of HMS Tribune, Captain Jeffrey Hornby, was not as impulsive despite his youth. Like Pickett, Hornby was in his 30s but had already served 22 years in the Royal Navy—yes, he joined at the tender age of 12. With his 31 guns pointed threateningly at Pickett's 64 infantrymen on the shore, Hornby was in a stronger position but chose a restrained approach. He was content to watch the Americans march up and down the beach, a response not anticipated by Governor Douglas, who subsequently sent two additional naval vessels, HMS Satellite and HMS Plumper—the latter having recently been part of the West Africa Squadron combating the slave trade—to San Juan.

Hornby, who would later command the West Africa Squadron and ascend to admiral of the fleet, was instructed by Douglas to deploy his raw marines to eject all Americans from the island, including Pickett's infantry. Hornby diplomatically declined, stating he would act only upon orders from Rear Admiral Robert Baines, the commander of the Royal Navy's Pacific station. Baines, a veteran who had entered service at 14 and fought in the Napoleonic Wars and the War of 1812, was also seasoned in naval battles from the Crimean War to the Greek War of Independence.

Admiral Baines, upon arriving at San Juan aboard the 84-gun HMS Ganges, was astounded by the escalation. The Americans had bolstered Pickett's garrison to 461 troops with 22 cannons, while the British had five naval ships, 2,000 men, and over 100 guns arrayed against them. Baines consulted with Governor Douglas in Victoria, who urged him to use his military superiority to force the Americans to capitulate. However, Baines refused to ignite a war over a trivial dispute about a pig, questioning the rationale behind escalating a minor territorial conflict into a full-blown confrontation.

As word of the tense situation reached President James Buchanan in Washington, D.C., he was equally concerned, particularly given the looming threat of secession in the United States. He promptly sent General Winfield Scott, another veteran of the War of 1812, to negotiate with Governor Douglas. Meanwhile, the bizarre stand-off continued with occasional gunnery practices by the Royal Navy, which even became a spectacle for civilians from Victoria. In an odd twist, American officers would join their British counterparts for church services aboard HMS Satellite.

When General Scott finally arrived in October 1859, negotiations still could not resolve the ownership dispute over the island. Nevertheless, it was agreed that the 55-square-mile island was not worth a war between two great nations over a pig, as Admiral Baines had asserted. Both sides agreed to maintain a token force of 100 men each on the island. The Americans established a camp at the island's south end, and 100 Royal Marines set up the English Camp at Garrison Bay.

Thus, the near-miss of the Pig War concluded with over a decade of coexistence between the garrisoned forces, marked by athletic matches, holiday celebrations, and occasional social drinking. During this period, Vancouver Island joined the Dominion of Canada, and the USA plunged into the Civil War, seeing George Pickett lead a notorious charge at Gettysburg. Post-war, ironically fearing prosecution, Pickett fled to Canada—the same country implicated in the earlier territorial dispute.

The ownership of San Juan Island was eventually settled by international arbitration under Kaiser Wilhelm I of Germany in 1872, determining that the island belonged to the USA. The British slowly withdrew, and by 1874, all American troops had also departed. Remarkably, the Union flag still flies daily at English Camp, a unique site in the USA where a foreign flag is regularly hoisted by government employees.

Thus ended the Pig War—a peculiar historical footnote where cooler heads like Admiral Baines and Captain Hornby averted what could have been a disastrous conflict, all sparked by a single pig.

Pope Formosus

Pope Formosus, known as Formosus I, served as the Pontiff of the Roman Catholic Church from 891 to 896. His pontificate was brief but eventful, marked by conflicts with the Holy Roman Emperor and controversies over the appointment of bishops. Despite being relatively obscure, Pope Formosus played a significant role in shaping the Catholic Church in the 9th century.

Born around 816 in Rome into a noble family, Formosus entered the clergy at a young age. In 864, he was consecrated as the Bishop of Porto, a city near Rome, where he served for approximately 25 years. During this time, he engaged in both political and religious affairs. As Bishop of Porto, Formosus made several bishop appointments without papal approval, leading to accusations of simony—selling divine favors and ecclesiastical offices.

Upon the death of Pope Stephen VI in 891, Formosus was unexpectedly elected his successor. Though not initially favored, he quickly established himself as a strong and decisive leader, implementing reforms, restoring clergy integrity, combating nepotism, and enforcing a stricter code of conduct for church officials. However, his tenure was fraught with difficulties, including poor management and constant conflicts with Holy Roman Emperor Arnold of Corinthia. Arnold, who had invaded Italy, sought to diminish the Pope's regional influence and pressured him to resign. Despite these challenges, Formosus's legacy in church history remains significant.

Formosus resisted Emperor Arnold's pressure, but their conflicts escalated. In 895, Arnold convened a council in Rome, accusing the Pope of perjury, treason, and simony. Formosus defended himself before a council largely composed of clerics appointed by Arnold, denied all charges, and was acquitted at the trial. However, after Formosus's death in 896, Arnold ordered the exhumation of his body for a posthumous trial. A newly convened council found Formosus guilty on all counts. His body was stripped of its pontifical garments and cast into a river.

The exhumation and posthumous trial of Formosus caused widespread scandal and outrage among church members and the broader society. Arnold's successor, Emperor Lambert of Spoleto, restored Formosus's reputation and condemned the actions of his predecessor.

Despite the difficulties of his pontificate, Pope Formosus left a significant legacy within the Catholic Church. He is remembered for his reforms, his defense of the Church's independence from secular authority, and his stand against simony. His martyrdom and the eventual restoration of his reputation highlight the Church's enduring power to challenge secular rulers. Today, while Formosus is primarily remembered for his exhumation and posthumous trial—one of the darkest episodes in Church history—his life and legacy represent much more. He was a courageous and determined leader who advocated for a more just and independent Church. Despite his brief and tumultuous life, his impact on the Church endures.

Einstein's Brain

Albert Einstein, the Nobel Prize-winning physicist renowned for his brilliance, had explicitly instructed that his body be cremated to prevent any form of idolization. Despite his fame, he disliked the idea of being memorialized or dissected for study. However, his death on the morning following his arrival at Princeton Hospital with a ruptured abdominal aortic aneurysm on April 17th, 1955, set off unexpected events.

The pathologist on duty, Dr. Thomas Stoltz Harvey, conducted an autopsy and, without any official direction, decided to remove Einstein's brain, presuming it would be subject to scientific scrutiny. Believing this would enhance his career, Harvey took the brain, preserved it in formaldehyde, and stored it at his home. This act was soon discovered by reporters, and it became clear that Harvey neither had the authorization nor the legal right to retain the brain.

When Einstein's son, Hans Albert, learned of this, he was deeply upset, given his father's clear wishes for cremation to avoid exploitation. This was the exact scenario Einstein had hoped to avoid. Nevertheless, Hans Albert eventually gave Harvey permission to keep the brain, but strictly for scientific purposes, with the stipulation that any findings be published in respected scientific journals.

Speculation arose that Harvey's actions were either at the behest of Harry Zimmerman, Einstein's personal physician and Harvey's mentor, who had requested the brain after its removal though never acknowledged doing so publicly, or that Harvey was possibly influenced by the famous study of Lenin's brain in 1926 and was overwhelmed by the moment.

Harvey hoped that analyzing Einstein's brain would significantly advance his career, though he was not a neurosurgeon or brain specialist. His role was solely to ascertain the cause of death, which was heart failure, and there was no directive to remove or study the brain. Despite Harvey's belief in the scientific value of preserving such a remarkable brain, his actions led him far beyond his expertise.

Who wouldn't be intrigued by the brain behind the theory of relativity, the photoelectric effect, and the equation $E=mc^2$? However, taking a brain without permission was bound to lead to significant consequences. Indeed, due to the controversy over the brain's unauthorized removal, Harvey lost his job.

With the brain in his possession, Harvey traveled to Philadelphia, where a specialized instrument called a microtome was used to slice the brain into 240 sections, which were then preserved in a gelatinous, rubbery substance called celloidin. Additional sections were preserved on slides, with some of the brain left whole. Harvey divided these pieces into two glass jars and stored them in his basement, where they remained unstudied for two decades.

In the mid-70s, Harvey and the brain relocated to Wichita, Kansas, where he worked as a medical supervisor in a biological testing lab, keeping the brain in a cider box beneath a beer cooler. In 1978, journalist Steven Levy, working for the New Jersey Monthly, was tasked with locating Einstein's brain. Levy ultimately found Harvey in Wichita, who admitted he still had the brain, stored in a box branded "Costa Cider."

Following Levy's article in August 1978, the media frenzy escalated, culminating in widespread coverage and interest from the scientific community. In 1984, Harvey sent samples of the brain to Dr. Marian Diamond at the

University of California, Berkeley. Unfortunately, the preservation method limited the potential for analysis, and any findings were likely compromised.

In 1985, Harvey and collaborators published a study suggesting atypical neuron and glial cell ratios in Einstein's brain. This study, along with five others noting cellular or structural anomalies, aimed to link these features to intelligence. However, these studies have since been largely discredited.

Harvey lost his medical license in 1988 after failing a competency exam and later moved to Lawrence, Kansas, where he worked in a plastic extrusion factory and befriended beat generation author William Burroughs. The two often socialized, with Burroughs boasting about having access to pieces of Einstein's brain.

In 1997, journalist Michael Paterniti arranged a trip with Harvey to take the brain to California, documenting the journey in the book "Driving Mr. Albert." After Harvey's death in 2007, his family held onto the brain until 2010, when they donated what remained, including photographs of the brain, to the National Museum of Health and Medicine in Silver Spring, Maryland.

While the scientific value of Einstein's brain remains contested, its cultural impact is undeniable, inspiring numerous articles, a play, a novel, and ongoing debate about Harvey's decision to keep the brain mostly to himself for 40 years rather than allowing it to be studied thoroughly. This saga stands as a poignant conclusion to the legacy of a man whose contributions fundamentally altered our understanding of the universe.

Confederates in Brazil

The American Civil War, a devastating and fierce conflict, resulted in the deaths of approximately 620,000 Americans, constituting about 2% of the population at that time. A key issue fueling the war was slavery, with the Southern states insisting that their state rights were being compromised. They sought to assert their dominance over the federal government and maintain the right to nullify federal laws, particularly those impeding the Southern right to own slaves. The election of Abraham Lincoln as president, who did not receive any Southern electoral votes, highlighted the perceived loss of Southern influence, prompting feelings of political alienation among the Southern states. This sense of exclusion ultimately drove them toward secession, a decision that directly sparked the war.

Following the Union victory, the Reconstruction era from 1866 to 1877 aimed to reintegrate the Southern states and set them on a path back to the Union. However, not all were ready to relinquish the practice of slavery. Former Alabama State Senator and dedicated Confederate, William H. Norris, along with his son, moved to Southeastern Brazil and bought 500 acres of land. They purchased three enslaved individuals, began cotton farming, and sent for their family to join them, continuing their lives as if the Confederacy had survived.

Many Confederates migrated post-war, with a significant number settling in Brazil, drawn by incentives from Emperor Dom Pedro II, a Confederate ally during the war. Dom Pedro offered land at low prices, subsidized transport, provided initial accommodations, fast-tracked citizenship, and even welcomed them personally. He aimed to attract Europeans and their descendants to "whiten" Brazilian society and enhance its agricultural sector with skilled farmers. The legality of slavery in Brazil, which had imported far more enslaved individuals than the U.S., was a major draw.

Confederate settlements sprang up across Brazil, from the Amazon in the north to Paraná in the south. However, many of these settlements were short-lived due to unsuitable soil for cotton, poor transportation infrastructure, and cultural barriers, including religious differences that prevented Protestants from burying their dead in Catholic cemeteries. Feeling homesick and isolated, many Confederates returned to the U.S.

However, Norris's settlement in Americana thrived, growing to include around 3,500 Confederates at its peak. Today, Americana has a population of over 200,000, with annual celebrations honoring its Confederate founders. The Confederate migration to Brazil remains a fascinating chapter in the aftermath of the American Civil War.

The Worst Video Game Ever Made

Atari, Inc., an American video game pioneer, transformed the U.S. perception of video games during the 1970s and '80s. Established by Nolan Bushnell and Ted Dabney in 1972, Atari's impact on gaming history is profound. The company originated as Syzygy—a term referring to a pair of connected or corresponding entities, symbolizing the founders' partnership. Initially, Bushnell and Dabney collaborated with Nutting Associates to develop a standalone arcade machine that operated on a coin slot, charging $0.25 per play. Facing challenges with Nutting, they then teamed up with Bally Manufacturing to create video game cabinets and pinball machines.

Their relationship with Bally was fruitful; they even offered Bally their next innovation, a game named Pong. However, Bally declined the offer. Undeterred, Bushnell and Dabney built their own Pong machine and tested it in a local Walgreens. The game was a hit, leading to installations in various bars and restaurants, each earning around $400 weekly.

In 1972, they officially formed Atari, Inc. The name "Atari," derived from the board game Go, signifies stones at risk of capture, akin to a critical defense stand. By 1973, Bushnell devised a strategy to navigate the gaming market, which was then dominated by pinball machines. To circumvent the exclusive rights demanded by pinball distributors, Bushnell launched Kee Games with his neighbor Joe Keenan. They would sell a pinball game under one name through Atari, then rebrand and sell it through Kee Games to another distributor, effectively doubling their profits. This strategy led to Keenan's promotion to president of Atari.

Steven Spielberg, widely regarded as one of the most successful commercial film directors of all time, rose to prominence in the New Hollywood era. He directed "ET the Extraterrestrial," one of the most influential films ever made. In the '60s and '70s, genre filmmaking, particularly involving science fiction and monster movies, was often dismissed. Spielberg transformed these genres, turning stories about aliens and gigantic creatures from mere campy tales into deeply human narratives that resonated emotionally and captured the hearts of a generation. "ET" not only normalized science fiction but also introduced a friendly alien character, transforming the typical alien invader trope into a story of friendship, which eventually led to a significant merchandising opportunity, including a video game.

In 1977, Atari introduced a home gaming console initially known as the Atari VCS, later renamed the Atari 2600. Priced at $199, it came with two joysticks and the game "Combat," selling about 375,000 units initially. However, 1978 saw a dip in sales; despite producing 800,000 units in anticipation of increased demand, only 550,000 were sold. Until then, Atari had developed all its games in-house but began to diversify by engaging third-party developers as the gaming industry grew. This included companies like Activision, founded by four former Atari employees, which produced iconic games like "Kaboom!" and "Pitfall!"

Atari continued to expand by securing licenses for popular arcade games, converting them for the 2600. One of the most successful was "PAC-MAN," developed by NAMCO, which generated nearly $10 million in cartridge sales. This strategy of adapting well-known arcade games proved lucrative for Atari. By the 1982 holiday season, Atari secured what they believed would be a highly profitable license: "ET the Extraterrestrial," inspired by Spielberg's blockbuster film.

Howard Scott Warshaw was considered one of Atari's most reliable talents when chosen to program the game.

After graduating from Tulane University, Warshaw joined Hewlett Packard as a multiterminal systems engineer. In 1981, Atari recruited him as a game designer and programmer. His first major success was "Yars' Revenge," initially envisioned as a remake of the arcade game "Star Castle." Warshaw reimagined it into a novel concept involving mutated houseflies battling alien invaders. Following this, he was tasked with adapting the iconic Spielberg film "Raiders of the Lost Ark" into a video game, which became a monumental hit and was the first video game based on a movie.

The challenge Atari presented to Warshaw with "ET the Extraterrestrial" was enormous. The project demanded quick execution as the game needed to be ready within six weeks to meet the holiday season release, under intense pressure since Atari was in desperate need of a successful launch. In the game, players controlled ET navigating fields full of pitfalls, using his alien powers to escape traps. Against all odds, Warshaw completed the game on time for the holiday rush.

Despite meeting the deadline, the game was a disaster, criticized for its difficulty and lack of connection to the film. It became known as the most significant commercial flop in video game history and was later dubbed "the worst game of all time." The release coincided with the video game market crash in 1983, often referred to in Japan as "the Atari shock," which lasted until 1985. This crash, driven by market saturation and a shift in interest from consoles to personal computers, along with the failure of "ET," led to Atari's downfall and eventual sale.

Rumors circulated that Atari disposed of millions of unsold "ET" cartridges by burying them in a New Mexico landfill. This urban legend persisted within the gaming community for years until Zak Penn, screenwriter of "X-Men 2" and "Hulk," decided to investigate. In 2014, he directed the documentary

"Atari—Game Over," which sought to uncover the truth. After extensive research, including interviews with former Atari employees and fans, Penn organized an excavation of the Alamogordo landfill on April 26, 2014. The excavation, attended by celebrities and fans, including Ernest Cline and Nolan Bushnell, confirmed the legend by uncovering the buried "ET" cartridges, thus solving one of gaming's most enduring mysteries.

CIA Spy Cats

From the debacle at the Bay of Pigs to the infamous misinformation about weapons of mass destruction in Iraq, the CIA has a history of costly and humiliating mistakes. Among the most outlandish was the 1960s' Operation Acoustic Kitty, a genuine initiative where CIA agents attempted to train a housecat as a spy.

The concept of a feline double agent wasn't even the strangest event during the tense 45-year nuclear standoff between the US and the USSR, which included plans like targeting hot dog stands with nuclear missiles and testing ejector seats on bears. Equipped with radio transmitters and microphones, the CIA hoped these cat spies would eavesdrop on secret discussions from window sills and park benches—classic hangouts for cats.

During the peak of the Cold War in the '60s, the CIA was desperate to monitor Russian activities in Washington, DC. Considering how people sometimes confide in their pets, the idea of using cats as spies didn't seem completely implausible.

Despite some pet owners spending heavily on their pets, the CIA went above and beyond, outspending even Karl Lagerfeld with a staggering $10 million (over $8 million in today's dollars) on training its hopeful feline spy. This hefty sum covered the development of implanted equipment, surgical procedures, and training to ensure the cat's cooperation—funded, of course, by taxpayer dollars.

To turn an ordinary house cat into a CIA double agent, agents implanted technological devices beneath its fur. Victor Marchetti, a former CIA officer, revealed the bizarre and costly details of this program in his book, "The Wizards of Langley." According to Marchetti, the agency surgically inserted batteries into the cat, using its tail as an antenna, creating a rather grotesque creature.

Cats, which generally detest baths, likely did not appreciate being transformed into something akin to Inspector Gadget. Despite their independent nature, which led to issues like wandering off during tests due to hunger, the cats' nonconformity posed a significant challenge to the CIA's structured spy program. But, after all, even spy cats need to eat.

Considering cats couldn't form unions and demand flexible lunch hours, the CIA attempted to address their wandering attention with an even more elaborate wiring system. It's puzzling why they thought additional mechanization would make the cats more cooperative. As mentioned earlier, this project was a complete flop from the start, without the luxury of multiple attempts to succeed.

Victor Marchetti shared with The Telegraph details about the rigorous testing process. When they noticed the cat would abandon its duties once hungry, they implanted another wire to suppress its appetite, suggesting the CIA might have inadvertently discovered a dieting secret far easier than calorie counting.

The transformation of the acoustic kitty from a playful house cat to a sleek, powerful CIA agent was an ordeal that went far beyond typical spy training montages seen in films. The extensive "spy kitty makeover" involved a brutal, hour-long surgical procedure—a nightmare scenario for any cat. As Emily Anthes describes in "Operation Acoustic Kitty," this included inserting a microphone into the cat's ear canal and a radio transmitter at the base of its skull, elevating pet body modification to extreme levels.

However, there was an unintended benefit: with a radio transmitter embedded, the cat could have enjoyed Andrew Lloyd Webber's *CATS* at full volume. The surgery also entailed implanting an antenna wire that integrated throughout the cat's fur, turning even its furry tail into an instrument of national security, significantly enhancing signal strength for transmitting recorded conversations.

If undergoing such extensive surgery, why not equip the cat with laser vision? It seems like a missed opportunity! CIA, if you're taking notes, our idea for a laser-equipped cat is up for grabs.

The concept of a half-cat, half-radio cyborg might have sounded solid theoretically, but it failed miserably in practice. Despite pouring millions of dollars and countless hours into this Cold War cat project, it unraveled rapidly during its initial live trial. After being released in a park to eavesdrop on a nearby conversation, the cat was tragically struck by a taxi while making its way back to the embassy, marking a swift and costly end to both the mission and its life.

Vincent Marchetti expressed their shock as they sat in the van, stunned by the sudden loss of their feline operative. The experiment not only challenged the notion that curiosity killed the cat—this time, it was a taxi.

Despite the enormous effort to establish a feline intelligence division, it was evident that cats had little interest in contributing to national security. The CIA only acknowledged this after extensive financial and temporal investments in training a distinctly uninterested spy. The project concluded abruptly, much like the cat's life, with a dry, somewhat humorous memo from the CIA stating that training cats did not meet their "highly specialized needs."

While dogs excel at various tasks supporting humans without technological enhancements, cats seem less inclined to stay even within their own yards.

However, should a conflict arise against a nation of mice, perhaps Operation Acoustic Kitty might see a revival.

Amid all the secrecy typical of espionage, there are conflicting accounts about the project's end. Robert Wallace, former director of the CIA's Office of Technical Service, contested the narrative of the cat's demise by taxi, suggesting instead that the cat was let go after several unsuccessful tests because cats are notoriously difficult to train. In his book "Beasts of War," Wallace claimed the cat lived a long, happy life post-experiment—a hopeful note, perhaps aimed at soothing critics.

As the military continues to draw inspiration from nature for its cutting-edge technology, including micro drones modeled after hummingbirds, the legacy of Operation Acoustic Kitty remains a peculiar yet fascinating chapter in the history of espionage.

Battle of Los Angeles

In the early hours of February 25, 1942, major cities along the Pacific Coast of the United States enacted blackouts due to concerns about an imminent enemy attack. As powerful searchlights scanned the sky, the normally bustling streets of Los Angeles became quiet. This quiet was soon shattered by loud explosions as the army began firing, believing the city was under attack. The blackout continued until dawn, leaving the populace anxious and demanding answers. However, there was no clear understanding of what had happened. Only shrapnel was found, and eyewitness accounts varied widely.

As World War II continued across the Pacific, this episode quickly faded from public memory. It later reemerged as a subject of conspiracy theories, with claims that the government had covered up the true events. This incident, known as The Battle of Los Angeles, has since become a key part of UFO mythology.

On December 7, 1941, the Imperial Japanese Navy unexpectedly attacked the American naval base at Pearl Harbor, causing widespread shock and leading the United States to declare war on Japan the next day. Following the attack, Japanese submarines patrolled the Pacific Coast, occasionally sinking ships visible from major cities. Alerts and blackouts became routine amid fears of a Japanese invasion. Less than three months after Pearl Harbor, Japan launched another attack on the US mainland.

On the evening of February 23, 1942, a Japanese submarine surfaced near Santa Barbara and fired on the Ellwood Oil Field. Although the damage was minor and there were no casualties, the attack heightened public fear of an invasion. Concerned that this might be a diversion, the military remained on high alert. The following evening, naval intelligence warned of a possible attack within ten hours, placing the southern California coast on Yellow Alert. Although the alert level was later downgraded, the threat of further attacks kept tensions high.

At 1:44 AM on February 25, radar stations detected an unidentified flying object approaching Los Angeles. By 2:00 AM, the target was detected offshore and antiaircraft batteries were prepared for an attack. Shortly thereafter, Los Angeles was blacked out and artillery units were ordered to open fire at 3:07 AM, causing the skies above to erupt violently. The firing continued sporadically, targeting a range of perceived threats from a single fighter to a fleet of up to 200 high-altitude bombers. Witnesses provided conflicting reports, with some seeing nothing and others mistaking aircraft for birds or balloons. Despite the continued blackout, the barrage ended around 4:00 AM after over 1,400 rounds of antiaircraft artillery had been fired.

The evening newspapers found it challenging to understand the events that had unfolded. Initial reports suggested that multiple enemy planes had been shot down over southwestern Los Angeles, with a police officer claiming to have seen two planes descend during the searchlight activity. Yet, local police investigations only turned up shrapnel, and the Western Defense Command confirmed that no bombs were dropped and no planes were shot down. This added to the confusion, as military officials did not agree on the events.

At a press conference in Washington, the Secretary of the Navy, Franklin Knox, declared the incident a false alarm, attributing the gunfire to nervousness and overexcitement rather than any real threat. On the other hand, the Secretary of War, Henry Stimson, believed that up to 15 unidentified planes had flown over the city, possibly as part of a Japanese reconnaissance mission or by enemy agents using commercial planes to instill fear and chaos. Despite efforts to clarify the situation, the American public received mixed explanations that ranged from potential threats to simple misidentifications.

As World War II ended in late 1945, declassified documents brought this nearly forgotten incident back into focus. An army investigation revealed through military and civilian testimonies that the firing had begun after a red flare attached to a balloon was seen above Santa Monica. The response included firing at various airborne objects such as balloons, airships, and airplanes, with one unit even reporting a plane caught on fire.

Despite these varied accounts, a conclusion on March 22 indicated that Japanese involvement was unlikely as no Japanese planes were near Los Angeles that night. The investigation, with FBI assistance, failed to find any corroborative evidence of enemy aircraft, leaving room for further speculation.

By 1948, a new theory emerged, researched by William Goss, a former Army Air Force Major and college professor, on behalf of the US Air Force. Goss had access to all relevant military records and concluded that weather balloons were likely responsible for the confusion, supported by the fact that the initial trigger for the barrage was a balloon carrying a red flare. At least three officers identified the target as a weather balloon, and one refrained from firing upon learning about the balloon's release by one of the regiments. This testimony was supported by a general who confirmed the release of two meteorological balloons near Hollywood that night. Some suggested that the slow movement observed was consistent with a balloon, which took nearly 30 minutes to cover approximately 40 km, a detail overlooked by the artillery units criticized for not considering the object's slow travel rate.

The balloon theory, while plausible, also raised questions about why the army would fire at a harmless balloon. A former Army Colonel, John Murphy, who was part of the investigation, provided insights into this reaction, suggesting possible reasons for the military's aggressive response.

In 1949, Murphy authored an article suggesting that when the Regional Controller in San Francisco was informed of a balloon over Los Angeles, he mistakenly thought it was a large enemy zeppelin and ordered to open fire without proper authorization. This action was somewhat supported by the army investigation.

However, a significant unresolved issue remains: how 1,400 rounds of antiaircraft ammunition failed to bring down a simple balloon. The lack of a clear answer to this and other questions provided ample room for conspiracy theories, suggesting that something extraordinary might have occurred. Adding to the intrigue, an LA Times correspondent, Bill Henry, reported that the UFO had withstood direct antiaircraft hits, though he later described the UFO as resembling a cluster of balloons.

The controversy deepened with a photograph published by The Los Angeles Times the morning after the event, which was later found to have been retouched. An earlier unpublished version showed no alterations, and another version published in 1945 featured flipped images and enlarged explosions, highlighting common photographic retouching practices of the time.

Despite these altered images showing light beams converging on something in the sky, what exactly that was remained unclear—it could have been a plane, a weather balloon, smoke, or even a spaceship. Other photographs from that night were similarly ambiguous, and none clearly showed a UFO.

The idea of a balloon withstanding extensive antiaircraft fire seems improbable unless it didn't. Murphy claimed both balloons released that night floated away safely. However, this was contradicted by an unnamed air raid warden who reported that the barrage focused on a large object resembling a balloon, which was eventually shredded by gunfire and fell to the ground.

Another simpler explanation might be related to the nature of weather balloons, which naturally ascend and move both horizontally and vertically, complicating their targeting. This scenario proposes that a weather balloon was mistaken for a zeppelin, triggering the barrage. Whether the balloon was destroyed by the shells or escaped by ascending is uncertain. Amidst the chaos, a second balloon could have been released, restarting the cycle, while the smoke from over a thousand explosions created illusions of multiple targets.

This confusion was further exacerbated by the Acting Commander's initial certainty of seeing a squadron of planes, later realized to be an illusion caused by drifting smoke. Historical analysis reveals that during World War II, such misinterpretations were common, exacerbated by inadequate radar equipment, which was critically assessed by British radar pioneer Robert Watson-Watt in early 1942 as unsuitable and likely to produce false tracks. Additionally, radar operators were not adequately trained, further complicating the detection and tracking of actual airborne objects.

The US Government Poisoned Alcohol

On the night before Christmas in 1926, over 60 individuals were admitted to a single hospital in New York City, suffering from severe illness and hallucinations. Within days, nearly half of them had perished. The culprit was not an infectious disease or tainted food, but rather alcohol tainted by the U.S. government—a fact that may sound like a conspiracy theory, but is indeed true.

During the 1920s, a lethal conflict unfolded between government officials and illicit alcohol vendors, leading to tens of thousands of poisonings and possibly up to a thousand deaths. Despite the Prohibition era, marked by jazz, flapper dresses, speakeasies, and lavish parties reminiscent of "The Great Gatsby," alcohol consumption persisted.

The 18th Amendment, enacted in 1920, prohibited the manufacture, sale, and distribution of alcoholic beverages, and remained in effect until its repeal in 1933. Many people continued to drink, often at great risk. With the black market as the only source, bootleggers frequently resorted to stealing industrial alcohol, which contained ethanol—a substance used in a variety of products from cosmetics to house paint.

To circumvent high import taxes on drinkable ethanol, the U.S. government began adulterating industrial alcohol with toxic chemicals in 1906, nearly 15 years before Prohibition. These additives included gasoline, chloroform, and methanol, making the alcohol undrinkable and exempt from the 18th

Amendment.

During Prohibition, bootleggers attempted to purify this alcohol through distillation, a process that removes impurities if done correctly. However, in 1926, under President Calvin Coolidge's directive, the government intensified its efforts by significantly increasing the methanol content, making the alcohol even more toxic.

Methanol, unlike ethanol, metabolizes into formaldehyde and then formic acid in the liver, disrupting cellular energy production and leading to severe health consequences, including digestive damage, vomiting of blood, kidney failure, and hallucinations—symptoms experienced by the victims in 1926. Methanol poisoning also risks permanent optic nerve damage, leading to blindness.

Despite the potential to remove methanol through careful distillation, the hurried conditions and substandard equipment of bootleg operations often failed to do so. The government's strategy indirectly led to thousands of deaths by 1933. Although not the intended outcome, these fatalities sparked significant political controversy.

As the decade ended, the government shifted to using less harmful additives that could not be removed by distillation. By 1930, new compounds like alcotate—a sulfurous compound with an unpleasant odor—were introduced. Although some industrial alcohol still contains methanol, such poisonings are now rare in the U.S., thanks to the lessened need to consume these dangerous substitutes post-Prohibition.

Antarctic Nazi Bases

In the mid-1930s, Hitler initiated a four-year plan aimed at revitalizing Germany's economy and military, with the nation gearing up for war. However, a significant challenge arose: despite Nazi Germany's ideology of self-sufficiency, it was heavily dependent on foreign nations for fats and oils. Margarine, a kitchen staple, was increasingly made with whale oil, a more affordable alternative to traditional ingredients. Whale fat, essential not only for food but also for war machinery and explosives, became a strategic asset. By 1930, German consumption of margarine had reached 17.12 pounds per person per year, making Germany the world's second-largest importer of Norwegian whale oil at approximately 200,000 metric tons annually. This reliance strained Germany's foreign currency reserves.

To address this issue, Hitler appointed Hermann Göring to lead the Four-Year Plan. Göring responded by developing the German Fat Plan to enhance domestic fat production, including butter, lard, and margarine. His plan led to the exploration of unclaimed Antarctic territories, specifically Queen Maud Land, for potential whaling operations and military bases. Helmut Wohlthat, a German State Counselor, had suggested this strategy to Göring.

The first German Antarctic exploration under this new plan took place in 1938-1939, aiming to map the territory aerially before establishing claims or selecting sites for a whaling station. This followed Germany's limited prior experience in Antarctica, marked by two significant but challenging expeditions.

The first, the Gauss Expedition in 1901 led by Erich von Drygalski, was primarily scientific. Despite hardships, including being trapped in ice, Drygalski's team conducted extensive research and made notable geographical discoveries. The second, led by Wilhelm Filchner in 1911, faced severe internal strife and external criticism, casting a shadow over its accomplishments despite discovering new territories.

As preparations for the third German Antarctic expedition began, led by Alfred Ritscher, the mixed legacy of the previous expeditions underscored the need for strong leadership and unity, particularly in Antarctica's harsh conditions. This expedition was not just about exploration but also about asserting Germany's strategic interests in the region.

By December 1938, following Göring's approval and initial preparations starting in May of the same year, the expedition officially set sail. The vessel, MS Schwabenland, named after the Swabia region in Bavaria, was a freighter built in 1925 designed to carry and launch aircraft. On January 19, 1939, it reached the Princess Martha Coast and began mapping the area. The expedition had dual purposes: it continued scientific research initiated earlier in the century and pursued covert military objectives, including testing aircraft performance in extremely low temperatures—vital for plans such as the anticipated invasion of the Soviet Union.

Just five days before the German team's arrival, Norway had claimed the area as Queen Maud Land through a royal proclamation. Despite this, the Germans proceeded with their plans, quickly setting up a temporary base and embarking on exploratory treks along the coast, marking territories at various natural landmarks. The region they charted was christened Neuschwabenland (New Swabia), named in honor of their ship.

Through oblique aerial photography, they mapped an area of approximately

250,000 square kilometers, extending between 11° West and 20° East. They discovered a new mountain range over 800 kilometers long and rising to heights of 3,000 meters, about 200 kilometers inland. These geographical findings had eluded the Norwegians during their previous expeditions.

The Germans strategically placed Nazi flags on the coastal sea ice to assert territorial claims and conducted seven photographic survey flights using the ship's seaplanes. These planes deployed nearly a dozen 1.2-meter-long aluminum arrows, each tipped with 30-cm steel cones and stabilizer wings marked with Nazi swastikas, embedding them into the ice at significant flight path points.

Additionally, eight targeted flights captured over 16,000 aerial photographs, some using color film, aided by favorable weather that was crucial for successful mapping. In February 1939, the expedition began its return to Germany, taking the opportunity to conduct oceanographic studies near Bouvet Island and Fernando de Noronha, and assessing potential landing sites for the German Navy on the remote Brazilian islands of Ilha Trindade and Ilhas Martin Vaz.

The MS Schwabenland reached Hamburg on April 11, 1939. Although the expedition expanded the explored area of Antarctica by 16%, Germany did not pursue the territorial claims due to the outbreak of World War II, which also halted planned expeditions for 1939-1940 and 1940-1941.

Post-war, any potential claims or plans for the region were abandoned with Germany's surrender and occupation. The secretive nature of the 1939 expedition to Queen Maud Land, coupled with the geopolitical upheavals of World War II and the early Cold War years, fostered a fertile ground for conspiracy theories and myths. Events like the unexpected arrival of two U-boats in Argentina post-surrender, the massive US Navy operation High Jump in Antarctica, and the classified detonations of three nuclear weapons during Operation Argus contributed to a complex web of speculation and mysterious narratives surrounding the region.

The first post-war event that fueled speculation occurred on July 10, 1945, when U-530, a German U-boat, docked at an Argentine naval base at Mar del Plata. Its captain, Lieutenant Otto Wermuth, seemed to expect a welcoming reception from the Argentinians, despite widespread news of Hitler's suicide on April 30th. This fueled rumors that U-530 had transported Hitler, Eva Braun, Martin Bormann, and others from Germany, possibly dropping them off in Patagonia or a secretive Antarctic refuge known as Neuberusgarten.

These rumors gained traction when Lisl Sabo, a Hungarian exile in Argentina, published a detailed narrative of Hitler's alleged escape and refuge in Queen Maud Land in the Argentine newspaper La Critica on July 6. The story quickly captured global attention, featuring in major newspapers, including a headline in the Toronto Star on July 18 that read "Hitler's on Ice in Antarctica."

Speculation intensified with the arrival of another U-boat, U-977, commanded by Heinz Schäffer, at Mar del Plata on August 17. Argentina, having joined the Allies at the end of the war, detained Vermuth, Schäffer, and their crews. They underwent extensive interrogation by the Argentine Navy, the US Navy, and the Royal Navy, focusing on whether Hitler or other high-ranking Nazis had escaped via submarine. The investigations ultimately found the delayed arrival of the submarines in the South Atlantic innocuous, leading to the eventual release of the U-boat commanders.

Despite these official findings, conspiracy theories persisted. In his 1947 publication "Hitler is Alive," Sabo claimed that these U-boats were part of a fleet tasked with transporting Nazi officials to Antarctica, where a base had been established under Admiral Dönitz's instructions during 1938-1939. Many authors have since propagated these theories, often contradicting each other or even themselves. For instance, Howard Bunér and Wilhelm Bernhard in their 1989 book "Hitler's Ashes: Seeds of a New Reich," suggested that Hitler perished in his Berlin bunker, but his remains, along with Nazi treasures, were transported to Antarctica and hidden in Queen Maud Land.

James Rob, in a 2005 series titled "Britain's Secret War in Antarctica," claimed that Bernhard was the captain of U-530, though his name does not appear on the crew list compiled by the Argentine Navy. Bernhard's alleged involvement is considered a fabrication by some, as his name is thought to be a pseudonym used by one of the crew members.

The concept of Neuberusgarten and the phantom convoy is largely attributed to Sabo's imagination but has been embraced by various authors as part of Nazi mythology. Some claim that US forces tried to attack this German stronghold during Operation High Jump in 1946-1947 but were repelled by advanced German weaponry, prompting an early retreat.

James Robert presents an alternate viewpoint, suggesting the existence of both secret German and British bases in Queen Maud Land during World War II. He alleges that the British Army's SAS attempted to destroy the German base around Christmas 1945, a mission that, along with subsequent American efforts during Operation High Jump, failed. He claims the German base was finally destroyed in 1958 through the secret detonation of three atomic bombs during the International Geophysical Year, accusing the US and British governments of concealing the truth about these events, which he calls "a travesty of history."

However, none of the German documents from the 1938 to 1939 period reference any plans to create a base during the expedition, nor is there any evidence that such an attempt was ever made. One author, Kristoff Friedrich, even manufactured evidence to support his claim in his 1979 book, "Germany's Antarctic Claim: Secret Nazi Polar Expeditions." He presented a photograph, allegedly showing a German aircraft on a frozen lake in Antarctica, which in reality depicted an ice shelf next to the ocean.

James Robert proposed a theory that a hidden Nazi base in extensive Antarctic caverns seemed plausible enough to prompt the British to establish several stations across Antarctica during World War II as a countermeasure. British forces were deployed as part of Operation Tabarin, primarily establishing outposts along the Antarctic Peninsula and nearby islands. Robert inaccurately suggested that an undocumented British base in Queen Maud Land called Maudheim was attacked by Germans in July 1945, leading to a SAS rescue mission during Christmas 1945. However, this claim is historically inaccurate as the war had ended over seven months earlier.

Operation Tabarin, initially classified, later became transparent through publications detailing its activities. The team departed from London in November 1943, reaching Antarctica by January 29, 1944. Their journey took them to Deception Island and other locations along the Antarctic Peninsula to set up bases for continued scientific research, aiming to bolster Britain's territorial claims post–World War II. In July 1945, Operation Tabarin transitioned to a civilian effort known as the Falkland Islands Dependency Survey.

Contrary to Robert's claims, historical records from 1947 show that five civilian British bases were operational in West Antarctica during Operation Highjump. Additionally, there's no credible evidence of an Operation Tabarin base on the coast of Queen Maud Land, as it was within Norwegian claimed territories, well outside the UK's jurisdiction.

Regarding the alleged SAS involvement, there is no evidence of SAS presence in the Falkland Islands in October 1945. A biography mistakenly suggested Lieutenant Colonel R.B. Main arrived in September 1945, but subsequent research corrected this to January 1946. Main, along with Majors J. Tonan and M. Sadler, both from the SAS and working under civilian contracts, helped establish and relieve bases, with Main returning to the UK in March 1946 due to health issues. Thus, there were no mysterious British operations in Antarctica during or immediately following World War II, nor was there a wartime base in Queen Maud Land or SAS deployment there.

Operation Highjump, conducted by the U.S. Navy after the war, is often misrepresented by authors who claim, without substantial evidence, that it aimed to destroy a hidden German base in Queen Maud Land. Bunér and Bernhard insinuate that the 1945 U-boat crew interrogations revealed extensive subterranean facilities in Antarctica for developing advanced aircraft and weaponry, suggesting Operation Highjump was a strategic response to this. However, the operation's scale and objectives, as stated in the U.S. Navy's report, included training personnel, testing equipment in frigid conditions, and investigating potential base sites, among others. The operation was a military exercise as part of the U.S. Navy's polar training initiative amid rising tensions with the Soviet Union, not a secretive military mission, as extensively documented with media coverage and journalist participation.

Although initially considered confidential, declassified comprehensive reports revealed there was no substantiation for claims of information suppression concerning a concealed Nazi threat. The recognized risk during this period stemmed from the Soviet Union, not from a hidden German base in Queen Maud Land as some theories suggested. The focus of Operation High Jump primarily targeted the region around Bird's Little America IV base on the opposite side of the continent, debunking claims that the operation's primary mission was to target a German base. The expedition mapped the Antarctic from the Ross Sea to the South Pole along the coastal areas, only briefly examining Queen Maud Land due to time constraints.

Speculations about the expedition ending prematurely due to hidden motives were dispelled by the actual circumstances that mirrored the duration of previous German expeditions to Antarctica, which were also cut short by harsh conditions. The expedition managed to meet most of its military goals despite losing an aircraft and its crew. This evidence counters conspiracy theories about a U.S. operation against a supposed German base in Queen Maud Land, indicating a lack of U.S. interest in the area.

The U.S. had shown interest in German activities in Antarctica due to concerns over territorial claims, which led to the formation of the U.S. Antarctic Service in 1939. Some authors, however, continued to propagate unverified theories, such as encounters with a German base equipped with advanced weaponry during Operation High Jump. These authors claimed significant losses of U.S. aircraft and personnel under mysterious circumstances involving enemy actions.

Nicholas Goodrick-Clark, in his 2002 book, discussed the evolution of the Nazi UFO claims starting in the 1950s, suggesting that German superweapons developed during the Third Reich might have been transported to remote regions post-war, leading to numerous UFO sightings attributed to a hidden Nazi presence. Despite these speculations, actual records and documentation from Operation High Jump showed that the primary areas of operation were far from Queen Maud Land, with no U.S. landings there and only a single aircraft lost on the other side of Antarctica.

The idea of flying saucers associated with Nazi technology gained traction in UFO circles, partly fueled by a supposed statement by Admiral Richard E. Bird, which was likely a mistranslation or misunderstanding, yet it has been repeatedly cited in various publications. Misinterpretations and deliberate fabrications by authors with dubious credentials have perpetuated a myth of Nazi resurgence involving advanced technology and hidden bases.

Further debunking these theories, official records indicate no nuclear detonations above Antarctica during Operation Argus, contrary to claims by some authors. The tests conducted were located significantly north of Queen Maud Land, and there was no unusual increase in radioactivity that would suggest otherwise. This absence of evidence, along with international scientific presence in Antarctica during the same period, strongly negates the possibility of concealed nuclear tests in the region.

Today, the narrative of a secret German base in Antarctica persists in some circles despite a lack of concrete evidence. No German documents have emerged to suggest continued Nazi activities in Queen Maud Land post-war. The notion that Hitler or his associates escaped to Antarctica is unfounded, and the actual purposes of operations like High Jump were focused on personnel training and equipment testing rather than combating a remnant Nazi force. The German activity in Antarctica did not resume until post-1959, culminating in the establishment of a permanent German research station in 1981. Control over the area remains under Norwegian governance, aligned with the Antarctic Treaty System.

Halifax Explosion of 1917

On December 6, 1917, two ships collided at the entrance of Halifax Harbour in Nova Scotia, Canada. The impact ignited a fire on a converted tramp steamer laden with explosives destined for the war in Europe. At precisely 9:04:35 a.m., this volatile cargo exploded, resulting in one of the largest non-nuclear blasts in history.

Halifax Harbour, situated on Canada's Atlantic coast, encompasses a vast enclosed bay called the Bedford Basin and a narrow strait known as The Narrows, leading out to the open sea and passing several small islands.

In 1917, the town of Halifax was located on one side of the harbour, and Dartmouth on the other. Together, they had a population of approximately 65,000, which had recently increased due to the ongoing First World War. The harbour's strategic importance made it a critical point for convoys heading to Europe, making it busier than ever.

Days before the catastrophe, the Norwegian ship SS Imo arrived and docked in the Bedford Basin, waiting for supplies, including coal, which was delayed. Cleared to depart on December 5, the Imo couldn't leave as submarine nets raised for the night blocked the passage to prevent German U-boat attacks.

Eager to depart, the Imo's crew had to wait until the following morning. Similarly, the French cargo ship SS Mont Blanc faced delays outside the harbour, unable to enter until the submarine nets were lowered the next day. The Mont Blanc, carrying a massive load of explosives including TNT, guncotton, picric acid, and barrels of benzol, remained outside, its crew undoubtedly wishing they were moored safely within the harbour.

On the morning of December 6, at 7:30 a.m., the nets were lowered, and both ships resumed movement—the Imo exiting and the Mont Blanc entering the harbour. Typically, vessels in The Narrows kept to the right and maintained a speed limit of five knots. However, the Imo's captain, in his haste, sped through at a significantly higher pace.

The Imo first encountered the SS Clara, an American tramp steamer, on the wrong side. After signaling each other, the Imo moved to the center to avoid a collision. Shortly after, it came across the tugboat Stella Maris in the middle of the strait and had to veer to the wrong side.

This maneuver placed the Imo directly in the path of the incoming Mont Blanc. Despite being over a kilometer apart, frantic signaling ensued. The Mont Blanc had the right of way, but the Imo's crew signaled their refusal to yield. As a collision became imminent, both ships cut their engines. The Mont Blanc attempted to steer clear, but the Imo, reversing its engines at a critical moment, caused its bow to strike the Mont Blanc.

The collision, though at low speed, was highly destructive and did not immediately sink either vessel. However, it ruptured several barrels of the Mont Blanc's flammable cargo, causing a significant spill of highly flammable materials.

Even then, disaster was not inevitable. Without a spark, even the most volatile materials remain inert. For a brief moment, the ships drifted apart after the Imo's engines restarted. As they separated, metal scraping against metal ignited a fire on the Mont Blanc.

Captain Aimé Le Medec of the Mont Blanc, recognizing the imminent danger, ordered his crew to evacuate. They quickly took to the lifeboats, rowing towards shore and shouting warnings to anyone in sight. However, amidst the cacophony on the water, few on nearby vessels or ashore could grasp the urgency of these alerts. The Mont Blanc, now aflame, drifted toward Halifax's side of The Narrows, eventually grounding near Pier 6. A towering smoke plume rose, drawing spectators from both sides of the harbor.

At precisely 9:04:35 a.m., the Mont Blanc's cargo exploded. The blast obliterated everything within 2.6 kilometers (1.6 miles) and caused extensive damage to thousands of buildings, with debris raining down over the city. A Mont Blanc deck gun landed 5.6 kilometers (3.5 miles) away. The shockwave, moving faster than sound, leveled buildings, uprooted trees, flipped cars, and displaced ships onto land. Approximately 1,600 lives were lost instantly, with many more injured.

The explosion also triggered a tsunami—a six-story wall of water that wreaked further havoc on those who had survived the initial blast, crushing and drowning many. The Imo, caught in the tsunami, saw nearly all aboard perish. Subsequent fires ignited by the disaster compounded the calamity, as collapsed boilers and overturned stoves set the debris ablaze.

Initially, the explosion was mistaken for enemy action due to the wartime context, leading to a delayed rescue response as soldiers manned their posts. Once the true cause was understood, a massive, somber rescue operation began. Firefighters, police, military personnel, and volunteers worked tirelessly, extracting survivors from the wreckage and rushing them to overwhelmed medical facilities.

The next day, a severe blizzard struck, compounding the city's misery with sub-zero temperatures and four feet of snow, hindering rescue efforts and blocking relief supplies. The Halifax Explosion, a multi-faceted disaster, claimed about 2,000 lives and left 9,000 injured.

An inquiry followed, initially blaming the Mont Blanc crew, a decision influenced by public anger and the higher survival rate of its crew compared to the Imo's. However, this ruling was overturned in 1919 by the Supreme Court of Canada, recognizing errors by both vessels.

Despite the tragedy, improvements in harbor navigation and hazardous material storage were implemented. The disaster also spurred the growth of charitable organizations like the Canadian National Institute for the Blind and reinforced the importance of the Red Cross in Canada.

In gratitude for assistance received, Nova Scotia began the tradition of sending a Christmas tree to Boston, which continues today. The disaster also led to the creation of the Hydrostone, one of Canada's first public housing projects, and cemented a lasting bond of friendship between Halifax and Boston.

Today, Halifax thrives as a maritime city, its population exceeding 400,000. While it has recovered, the Halifax Explosion remains an integral part of its history, a reminder of both the tragic past and the resilient spirit of its people.

Charles Joughin

Charles Joughin was born on August 3, 1878, in Birkenhead, Cheshire, England. The son of a licensed victualler, essentially an innkeeper, he grew up with four siblings. Records from 1900 and 1901, when he was 22, show that he worked as a baker aboard the RMS Majestic and later on the RMS Teutonic. His brothers served in the Royal Navy; one, Theodore, died on the RMS Cornwallis on March 1, 1915, and was buried at sea.

Charles married Louise Woodward on February 11, 1907, and they had a son and a daughter. He was on the Titanic's delivery trip from Belfast to Southampton and was promoted to Chief Baker during this journey, earning 12 pounds per month, equivalent to about $470 today. He managed a galley staff of 13, including 10 bakers, two confectioners, and a van Anna Baker, who specialized in breakfast pastries.

On the night of April 14, the collision with the iceberg woke Charles. Without official orders, he rallied his staff to bring bread and provisions to the lifeboats. After doing so, he returned to his cabin for a drink. By 12:30 a.m., he was on the boat deck, where he observed and aided Chief Officer Wilde in calmly boarding women and children into Lifeboat 10. After ensuring it was only half-full, he and other crew members sought more passengers to fill it.

Believing no lifeboats remained later that night, Charles began throwing deck chairs off the second-class promenade to use as flotation devices. He then made his way to the poop deck as the Titanic sank, claiming a spot at the stern railing. Contrary to cinematic portrayals, he maintained that the ship didn't reach a vertical position and that he was nearly alone during the final moments.

A strong swimmer, Charles tread water until dawn when he was recognized by Isaac Mayard on an overturned collapsible boat and later rescued by another lifeboat, eventually being taken aboard the Carpathia. Despite the freezing conditions, which typically would induce cardiac arrest or hypothermia within minutes, he only suffered from swollen feet, perhaps aided by alcohol, contrary to scientific expectations.

After the Titanic, Charles returned to his family in England, then moved permanently to New Jersey, USA. He continued working on ships throughout World War II, including on the SS Oregon, which also sank in 1941. He passed away on December 9, 1956, after over 50 years at sea. His experience on the Titanic has been depicted in two major films, highlighting his alertness and sobriety during the disaster. His actions and survival story remain well recognized.

Starfish Prime

On July 9, 1962, at precisely 09:00:09 Coordinated Universal Time, the Starfish Prime test was conducted at an altitude of 400 kilometers (about 250 miles), with the detonation occurring nine seconds past 10 p.m. local time on July 8 at Johnston Island. The explosion took place at coordinates 16 degrees, 28 minutes north latitude, and 169 degrees, 38 minutes west longitude, approximately 30 kilometers (18 miles) southwest of Johnston Island. The yield of the explosion closely matched the expected range of 1.4 to 1.45 megatons (6.0 PJ).

The test involved a Thor missile carrying the nuclear warhead to an apogee of approximately 1100 kilometers (over 680 miles). The warhead was then detonated on its downward trajectory at the designated altitude of 400 kilometers. This event occurred 13 minutes and 41 seconds after the Thor missile was launched.

Starfish Prime generated an electromagnetic pulse (EMP) significantly stronger than anticipated, overwhelming much of the measuring equipment. This extensive EMP also publicly revealed its potent effects by causing electrical disruptions in Hawaii, nearly 1,445 kilometers (900 miles) from the detonation site. The impact in Hawaii included knocking out around 300 streetlights, triggering numerous burglar alarms, and damaging a telephone company's microwave link.

In preparation for the test, 27 sounding rockets were launched from Johnston

Island to gather experimental data, with the initial support rockets launched two hours and 45 minutes before the Thor missile. Concurrently, a considerable array of rocket-borne instruments was launched from Barking Sands, Kauai, in the Hawaiian Islands.

Supporting the operation were numerous U.S. military ships and aircraft in the Johnston Island region and the broader North Pacific area, including the USAS American Mariner, which provided primary instrumentation measurements through personnel from RCA Service Company and Barnes Engineering Company. Observation ships from the Soviet Union, uninvited, were also present near Johnston Island and in the southern conjugate region during the test.

Following the detonation, vivid auroras were observed near the detonation site and in the southern conjugate region across the equator. The burst illuminated a vast expanse of the Pacific, enhancing visibility for various military operations, including Royal New Zealand Air Force anti-submarine maneuvers.

The radiation belt created by Starfish Prime lingered in the high atmosphere for months, adversely affecting several satellites, including American and Soviet ones, many of which failed within months of the event. A 2010 report by the United States Defense Threat Reduction Agency detailed the extensive satellite damage caused by these artificial radiation belts and analyzed the potential impact of contemporary high-altitude nuclear explosions on current satellite operations.

The Erfurt Latrine Disaster

July 25th, 1184, in Erfurt, Duchy of Thuringia, found Louis III, a Landgrave akin to a duke within the Holy Roman Empire and a nephew of the Emperor himself. Unlike routine meetings, this gathering at the Petersberg Cathedral was a crucial mediation mandated by the Emperor to resolve a dispute between Louis and his neighboring foe, Archbishop Conrad. Facilitated by the Emperor's son, the King of Germany, Louis likely approached the meeting with a mix of dread and curiosity, wondering about its duration and if a lunch or at least a bathroom break would be included.

Indeed, a bathroom break did occur—one that would significantly impact his life and nearly alter the Holy Roman Empire's course.

As a Landgrave of Thuringia, a sovereign region under the Holy Roman Empire, Louis did not possess a throne but a prestigious chair. From this seat, he had watched with growing concern the aggressive actions of Conrad, Archbishop of Mainz. Conrad's construction of a fortified castle at Louis's border was a clear threat, emerging during a time when territories frequently changed hands through dynastic trades or local skirmishes.

First appointed to the bishopric of Mainz in 1160, Conrad spent about 20 years in exile after clashing with Emperor Frederick Barbarossa over ecclesiastical appointments, specifically rejecting the Emperor's nominee for antipope—a deeply personal and significant affront. Upon his return, Conrad wasted no time in expanding Mainz and restoring its former stature, enhancing his political influence significantly.

When Louis voiced objections to Conrad's territorial ambitions, he pondered whose side the Emperor would take—his loyal nephew Louis or the politically adept Conrad, known for hosting grand feasts like the Diet of Pentecost. The Emperor's decision not to pick a side stung Louis, leaving him to face the possibility of open conflict.

With tensions escalating, the Emperor dispatched his son, Henry, the King of Germany, to mediate between Louis and Conrad at Erfurt. The meeting attracted considerable attention, with over 60 nobles taking time from their schedules to witness the resolution of the land dispute—an event of significant interest in a pre-television era. Among the observers were notable figures such as Count Frederick of Kirchberg, Count Burkhardt of Wartburg, and Count Henry of Schwarzberg, whose presence added to the anticipation of the historical mediation.

Henry of Schwarzberg was hardly a neutral spectator at the meeting in Erfurt, particularly from Louis of Thuringia's perspective, given their tumultuous past. Indeed, Louis had initiated their discord by burning down Henry's castle. To add a twist, please note the presence of two Henrys in this tale: remember, King Henry is the one wearing a crown. In a bold act of retribution, on the night of Louis's wedding, non-king Henry allegedly pilfered a unique German courtly romance manuscript derived from Virgil's Aeneid. Although the evidence pointed to him, Henry never confessed to the theft. This accusation surely soured Louis's mood as he approached the significant gathering at Petersburg Citadel in Erfurt, joining King Henry, his adversary Conrad, the supposed thief Henry, and numerous other nobles within the ancient walls of Saint Peter's Church.

This church, modest and aged, was not designed to support the weight of a king, numerous princes, and their entourages. As the assembly commenced, the old wooden floor, strained under the collective weight, gave way, plunging over sixty princes, including Louis, into the cellar below which doubled as a latrine. The phrase "cellar door" may be considered beautiful, but crashing through to a cellar latrine is anything but, especially as many met their fate upon impact or succumbed to the toxic fumes.

Among the victims was Henry of Schwarzberg, potentially taking the secret of the stolen manuscript to his untimely grave. Meanwhile, Louis found himself struggling in the depths of monastic waste, witnessing King Henry and Archbishop Conrad, who had managed to avoid the fall, dangling precariously over the pit. This incident highlighted the dangers of medieval waste disposal systems, which were effective only until disrupted by such catastrophic accidents.

Rescue efforts were swift for the nobles who remained above, including King Henry, who departed promptly post-rescue, unwilling to endure the aftermath of nearly drowning in waste. The meeting disintegrated thereafter. Remarkably, Louis survived, but the dramatic incident at Erfurt dissuaded the Emperor and his son from further meddling in the dispute between Louis and Conrad. This disaster unfolded just as the Third Crusade was about to commence, led by Emperor Barbarossa who would meet his own watery demise.

Post-crisis, Archbishop Conrad's influence continued to grow, while Louis, reflecting on his life post-near death experience, joined the Crusade, only to fall ill and die on a ship surrounded by the clean water he had so desperately missed at Erfurt.

Before his departure, however, a conciliatory gesture came from the brother of Henry of Schwarzberg, who returned the stolen manuscript to Louis, a poignant closure to their longstanding conflict. Thus, despite the disastrous meeting at Erfurt, Louis ultimately reclaimed his prized possession, settling the score with his adversary in an unexpected yet effective manner. This tale serves as a reminder that history often remembers those who survive its most dire events, not those who perish in them.

Major William Martin

Huelva is a modest town in southwest Spain, close to the Portuguese border. Just outside the town is the town cemetery, located in the San Marco section, where a grave stands out from the rest. This grave bears a British name, "William Martin," which is the alias of Glendal Michael, a Welshman who played a pivotal role in a wartime deception. Born to John Glendora Martin and Antonia Martin of Cardiff, the grave also marks the death of Glendal Michael on April 24, 1943. The story of how he came to rest here is a tale of wartime subterfuge.

Rewind to January 1943 in Casablanca, Morocco, where Winston Churchill and Franklin D. Roosevelt agreed to launch Operation Husky, the invasion of Sicily. To mislead the German High Command about the invasion's location, British intelligence, led by Flight Lieutenant Charles Chumley and Royal Naval Officer Captain Ewan Montague, initiated Operation Mincemeat. They acquired the body of Michael, who had died from ingesting rat poison, and transformed him into the fictitious Major William Martin. They equipped the body with personal items, letters, and a crucial set of documents intended to mislead the Germans about the Allies' plans.

These documents suggested that the Allies considered reinforcing positions in Greece and Crete, diverting German resources. The body, dressed in Royal Marine officer's uniform, was placed in a sealed container with dry ice and transported by submarine HMS Seraph to southwest Spain. Released into the sea, the body was discovered by Spanish fishermen, setting the deception in motion.

The Spanish, upon finding the body, conducted a hasty post-mortem pushed by the British Council and buried him with full military honors on May 2, 1943. The Spanish sent the discovered briefcase to Madrid, avoiding direct handover to the Germans. German intelligence, led by Admiral Wilhelm Canaris, inspected the documents but the Allies had already planted seeds of misinformation, leading the Germans to move their forces to the Balkans.

On July 9, the Allies launched their attack on Sicily, facing significantly fewer casualties and naval losses than anticipated, partly thanks to the misdirection of Operation Mincemeat. The grave was officially recognized by the Commonwealth War Graves Commission in 1977, and it was publicly disclosed in 1996 that the grave belonged to Glendal Michael. In 1997, the inscription acknowledging his role as Major Martin was added. While much about Michael's life remains unknown, his posthumous service significantly impacted the war effort.

Goldsboro Incident

The incident now referred to as the Goldsboro Incident occurred on January 23, 1961, when a B-52 Stratofortress, flying over the Atlantic near the U.S. coast, experienced a fuel leak. The crew was directed to head towards Seymour Johnson Air Force Base near Goldsboro, North Carolina, for an emergency landing. As the plane transitioned over land, control was lost, forcing the crew to bail out. Only five of the crew members successfully parachuted to safety; the others perished in the crash.

This was no ordinary flight, as the aircraft was carrying two 3.8-megaton thermonuclear bombs. After control was lost, the aircraft broke apart, causing the bombs to be ejected over North Carolina. Fortunately, neither bomb detonated. The next morning, investigators discovered one bomb with its parachute deployed and the other had crashed into a forest, burying itself 18 feet underground. Despite the high potential danger, the weapon cores did not rupture and no radiation was released.

At the time, the military worked to maintain public calm, but later records revealed that there was significant concern over the possibility of accidental detonation. This fact only became widely known in 2013, when author Eric Schlosser obtained documents through the Freedom of Information Act. These documents revealed that five of the six safety mechanisms on one bomb had failed during the fall. It was only a single low-voltage switch from the 1960s that prevented a catastrophic explosion. To put the potential devastation into perspective, each bomb was 250 times more powerful than the one dropped on Hiroshima.

The incident sparked a debate among researchers regarding the likelihood of detonation, with some arguing that additional safety mechanisms would have prevented the bombs from exploding. Nonetheless, the 1961 incident remains a stark reminder of the risks associated with nuclear armaments. This was one of 700 significant nuclear mishaps recorded between 1950 and 1968, highlighting a perilous era of nuclear safety. Remarkably, a significant piece of enriched uranium from the bomb that landed without a parachute has never been recovered.

Lincoln Hall

Lincoln Ross Hall OAM, born in Canberra, began rock climbing at 15, driven by a fascination with a world that demanded sharp focus, precise judgment, and a readiness to take risks. Educated in Zoology at the Australian National University, he joined the mountaineering club and successfully summited peaks in New Zealand, the Andes, and beyond. Also an accomplished author, Hall wrote notable books on mountaineering, including the classic "White Limbo." A prominent figure in Australian mountaineering, he was part of the first Australian Everest expedition in 1984.

Despite an initial failure to reach the summit in 1984, Hall was invited back to Everest in 2006 at age 56. During this ascent, he faced dire conditions that led to the tragic death of British climber David Sharp near the summit, which deeply affected Hall. However, he reached the summit but suffered cerebral edema during his descent, causing severe hallucinations and fatigue. Left for dead, Hall miraculously survived the night at over 28,000 feet without oxygen or proper clothing. Found alive the next day by climber Dan Mazur and his team, Hall's survival became legendary.

Despite severe frostbite and health issues, Hall managed to speak to his wife from Everest. He later succumbed to malignant mesothelioma in 2012, a disease he developed from exposure to asbestos during his childhood. His gear is displayed at the Australian National Museum, a testament to his remarkable story and contributions to mountaineering. Watch to discover more about how Lincoln Hall made history by surviving a perilous night on Everest and his impactful life thereafter.

Lady Wonder Psychic Horse

Lady's story begins on a chilly day in February 1924. Just weeks after she came into the world, a filly with a coat as dark as the night sky was adopted by Clarence and Claudia Fonda, who named her Lady. In the comfort of their home, Lady was not just another pet; she was a member of the family. Claudia, with a nurturing touch, bottle-fed the young horse, fostering a bond that blurred the lines between human and animal.

Intrigued by Lady's keen intelligence, Claudia embarked on an ambitious endeavor—she introduced Lady to children's wooden blocks, each adorned with letters and numbers. This was no mere game; it was an attempt to breach the communicative divide between species. As Lady grew, so did her understanding, but soon, the blocks were too small for her burgeoning curiosity.

Observing this, Clarence constructed a large typewriter specifically for Lady. This device, a marvel of homespun engineering, featured padded keys large enough for Lady's nose to press. Each key was connected to a tin card, lifting to reveal a letter or number, allowing Lady to 'speak' to her human companions. Over the years, this remarkable contraption drew over 150,000 visitors from across the United States, all eager to witness Lady's communicative prowess.

Lady's fame wasn't just due to her unique method of communication. She became known for her predictions, which ranged from boxing matches—like Gene Tunney's victory over Jack Dempsey in 1927—to shifts in the stock exchange and impending earthquakes. Her prognostications even extended to U.S. presidential elections, where she maintained an almost flawless record, only missing the unexpected result of the 1948 election when Truman triumphed over Dewey.

However, not all viewed Lady's abilities through a lens of wonder. Skeptics pointed to errors and the potential for human interpretation in her predictions. Despite the controversy, Lady remained a beloved figure until her peaceful passing from a heart attack on March 19, 1957, at the age of 33. She was laid to rest in the Pet Memorial Park in Henrico County, leaving behind a legacy wrapped in mystique and affection.

As Lady's fame blossomed throughout the United States, one incident in particular underscored her extraordinary abilities and thrust her further into the national spotlight. In Quincy, Massachusetts, the case of Danny Matson, a four-year-old boy who had vanished without a trace, was growing cold. Desperate for any lead, the local authorities turned to Lady. When asked where Danny could be found, Lady tapped out a cryptic message: "Pittsfield Water Wheel." Baffled, the police scoured records and maps of Pittsfield, Massachusetts, only to confirm there was no such water wheel in existence.

Undeterred, Police Chief William Ferrazzi pondered Lady's message, suspecting a misinterpretation. He considered the possibility that Lady was referring to "Field and Wilde Water Pit," a quarry not far from the Matson home and a site previously searched by the authorities. Compelled by Lady's clue, they conducted a more thorough search of the quarry. Tragically, it was there they discovered young Danny's body.

Several years later, in December 1952, another chilling case emerged in Naperville, Illinois. Two children had disappeared, vanishing near their home. In desperation, the mother of one of the boys sought Lady's insight. With her usual solemn demeanor, Lady suggested that the children would be found at the DuPage River, which flowed near where the children had last been seen. Despite initial searches yielding no results, the grim discovery of both children's bodies over the frozen river came several weeks later.

In both instances, skeptics were quick to note that the locations identified by Lady had already been under scrutiny by the authorities. Critics argued that Lady's contributions merely echoed the ongoing thoughts of the search parties rather than providing new insights. Nevertheless, for those who believed, Lady's involvement reinforced their faith in her mysterious abilities, cementing her status as a figure of intrigue and wonder in American folklore.

In the cold winter months of 1927–1928, the mysterious capabilities of Lady Wonder captivated J.B. Rhine, a pioneering researcher of extrasensory perception. Rhine embarked on a series of tests to explore the extent of Lady's psychic prowess. His findings were both unexpected and groundbreaking: there was no detectable conscious or unconscious signaling from the researchers or Mrs. Fonda. Rhine concluded that the only plausible explanation for Lady's abilities was telepathy.

However, a subsequent examination in December 1928 painted a different picture. Rhine observed a noticeable decline in Lady's telepathic abilities, discerning that her responses now seemed to rely significantly on cues from Mrs. Fonda. This shift suggested a deeper complexity or perhaps a manipulation of the phenomena previously attributed solely to Lady.

By 1956, skepticism around Lady's abilities had grown, attracting the attention of Milbourne Christopher, a magician with a keen interest in debunking psychic phenomena. Christopher, under the alias John Banks, visited the Fondas with a plan to challenge the authenticity of Lady's talents. Upon his inquiry, Lady correctly spelled out "Banks," a response that piqued Christopher's suspicions. To probe further, he employed a technique known as pencil reading—a method where mentalists predict answers by observing the writing movements of the questioner. Christopher cleverly manipulated this test by mimicking the motion of writing the number 9, while only making contact with the paper in a manner that would produce the number 1. When Lady responded by spelling out "9," it seemed to confirm Christopher's theory that Mrs. Fonda was guiding Lady's answers through subtle cues.

This revelation was paralleled by the investigations of another magician, John Scarne from New Jersey. Scarne, too, concluded that Lady's performance was not independently derived but heavily influenced by Mrs. Fonda's guidance, particularly when she held a whip. Whenever Mrs. Fonda was unaware of the correct response, Lady's answers tended to be incorrect, reinforcing the belief that the enigmatic horse's "psychic" abilities were orchestrated rather than genuine. These examinations cast a shadow of doubt over the once-celebrated narrative of Lady Wonder, suggesting a clever interplay of human influence rather than a marvel of animal telepathy.

Nicholas Alkemade

In March 1944, Nicholas Alkemade, a Royal Air Force tail gunner, was aboard his Lancaster heavy bomber when it was struck by German flak. His parachute ignited, leaving him with seemingly no chance of survival as his burning aircraft spiraled out of control. As flames engulfed his clothing, Alkemade faced a dire choice: "I had no doubt at all that this was the end of the line. The question was whether to stay in the plane and burn or jump to my death. I decided to jump and make a quick, clean end of things." He somersaulted out of the turret and, hours later, miraculously opened his eyes to a new dawn, cigarette in hand, savoring his unlikely survival.

Nicholas Stephen Alkemade, born on December 10, 1922, in Norfolk, United Kingdom, was a market gardener before joining the war. He became a rear gunner for the Avro Lancaster bombers of the 115th Squadron. After completing 14 missions, his crew was tasked with raiding Berlin on March 24, 1944. Their aircraft, nicknamed "Werewolf," was part of a fleet of 811 planes targeting the German capital. On their return, strong winds pushed them over a heavily defended area. Just before midnight, their Lancaster was attacked from below, causing catastrophic damage.

As flames engulfed the aircraft, pilot James Newman ordered the crew to bail out. Trapped in the cramped rear turret without a parachute, Alkemade attempted to retrieve one from a storage locker only to find it ablaze. With his oxygen mask melting and his face searing, he faced a grim decision. Choosing to jump from 18,000 feet, he somersaulted into the night, expecting death but finding peace in his final thoughts.

Miraculously, Alkemade awoke hours later on a snow pile, mostly unscathed except for minor burns and a twisted knee. Surrounded by soft pines that cushioned his fall, he lit a cigarette and pondered his incredible luck. His boots were gone, and nearby, an area free of snow hinted at how differently things could have ended.

Alkemade, freezing and unable to walk, discarded his parachute harness and blew his distress whistle. Soon, local Germans discovered him and took him to an infirmary, later transferring him to a proper hospital. There, he was treated for his burns, cuts, and removed splinters. Despite the ordeal, he emerged virtually unscathed. The next day, Gestapo agents arrived to interrogate him, skeptical of his claim of not using a parachute and suspecting him of espionage—a charge that carried the death penalty. Alkemade stood firm, challenging them to find his harness. The Germans eventually discovered the unused parachute 20 miles away in the "Werewolf" wreckage, still in its container with intact ripcord and cables. Impressed, they awarded him a certificate acknowledging his miraculous survival from an 18,000-foot fall without a parachute, landing safely in deep snow among fir trees.

After three weeks in the hospital, Alkemade was sent to a prisoner of war camp in Poland, where he spent the last 14 months of the war. During this time, he became somewhat of a celebrity among the prisoners, often receiving extra cigarette rations. Fellow prisoner Flight Lieutenant Bennett Kenyon even painted his portrait. As the war neared its end and the Russians approached, the Germans initiated a massive evacuation of prisoners known as "The Long March," during which Alkemade survived harsh conditions and a perilous journey to northern Germany.

Of the seven-man crew of the "Werewolf," only three survived the war, including Alkemade, navigator Sergeant John Cleary, and wireless operator Jeffrey Burwell. Post-war, Alkemade appeared on the ITV series "Just Amazing," which featured individuals with incredible survival stories, interviewed by former motorcycle racer Barry Sheene. Discharged from the Royal Air Force in 1946, Alkemade then worked in a chemical plant, where he survived several accidents, including severe electric shocks and exposure to sulfuric acid, which he neutralized by diving into a limewash drum. His final job was as a furniture salesman in Loughborough, where he lived with his wife and children until his peaceful passing in 1987 at the age of 64.

Helen Duncan

Victoria Helen MacFarlane, commonly known as Helen Duncan, was born on November 25, 1897, in Callander, Scotland. Her father, Archibald McFarlane, worked as a cabinet maker or slater, while her mother, Isabella Rattray, was a typical housewife of that era. From an early age, Helen exhibited a pronounced spiritual inclination.

During her school years, Helen was known for her hysterical behavior and her unsettling predictions that frightened her peers. Though these actions did not cause her significant trouble, they certainly did not please her mother Isabella, a member of the local Presbyterian Church.

Like many children from working-class backgrounds, Helen left school at the age of 12 and soon after began working at Dundee Royal Infirmary. She continued living with her parents until marrying Henry Duncan in 1916, when she was 20 years old. Henry, a cabinet maker and a wounded veteran of the First World War, supported Helen's paranormal abilities.

After marrying, Helen became pregnant twelve times, enduring several miscarriages and infant deaths, with only six children surviving. To supplement the family's income, she worked part-time in a local bleach factory and handled household duties. During this period, she maintained her spiritual practices and started conducting séances to earn extra money. Helen, now a physical medium, was reputed to materialize spirits of the deceased.

Throughout the 1930s and 1940s, Helen's fame grew as she traveled across Britain, conducting séances attended by hundreds from various social strata, including spiritualists, ordinary folk, and academics. These sessions often induced a trance state in attendees, followed by the appearance of ectoplasm from Helen's mouth, shaping into figures of deceased individuals who could interact with their living relatives. This brought immense solace to many families grieving the massive casualties of the world wars.

Among the many accounts of Helen's séances, one notable story involves Vincent Woodcock, whose wife had recently passed away. At one séance, Helen, in a trance, produced a spirit that took the form of Woodcock's late wife, who then enacted a symbolic gesture of passing her wedding ring to her sister, expressing a wish for Woodcock to marry her sister for the sake of their daughter. Woodcock later married his sister-in-law, and they received a spiritual blessing in a subsequent séance.

However, Helen's career was not without controversy. In 1928, a photographer named Harvey Metcalfe attended her séances to capture the truth behind her materializations. His flash photography supposedly exposed some of the spirits as fabrications, like a doll crafted from a painted papier-mâché mask draped with an old sheet.

Further scrutiny came in the early 1930s when the London Spiritualist Alliance investigated her methods, amid claims that she produced ectoplasm by regurgitating cotton cloth, sometimes purportedly stored in her nose to explain frequent nosebleeds during séances. An experiment involving Helen ingesting methylene blue was conducted to see if any regurgitated material would be stained, thus indicating fraud. Results were mixed, with some observers reporting no ectoplasm, while others claimed she still produced pristine, white ectoplasm.

Until then, it had been uncertain how genuine Helen Duncan's practices were, yet people from across the country continued to attend her séances. Around the same period, psychic researcher Harry Price paid Duncan £50 to conduct test séances with the goal of exposing her as a fraud. In his report, Price described a tumultuous scene: after being presented with an X-ray machine, Duncan, initially resisting the procedure, entered a trance and subsequently erupted into violent behavior, assaulting her husband and attempting to attack Dr. William Brown. Fleeing into the street in hysteria, she tore at her séance attire and caused a public disturbance that attracted police attention. Once back in the laboratory, she inexplicably agreed to the X-ray.

Price also documented evidence of fake ectoplasm composed of cheesecloth, rubber gloves, and magazine cutouts, which Duncan claimed were spirits. Her former maid, Mary McGinlay, admitted to assisting in these deceptions, and Duncan's own husband confirmed the fraudulent nature of the ectoplasm. Despite these revelations, Duncan's séances persisted. In 1933, a séance exposed a supposed spirit as merely a stockinette undergarment, infuriating her audience and leading to her arrest and a conviction for fraudulent mediumship, resulting in a fine.

Demand for Duncan's services surged with the onset of World War II, as people sought to connect with deceased loved ones. However, her knowledge of the HMS Barham's sinking—information that was supposed to be confidential—drew naval attention. In January 1944, naval officers unimpressed by her séance reported her, leading to a raid and her arrest for vagrancy. Despite it being a minor charge, authorities were determined to secure a harsher sentence, leading to her incarceration in London's notorious Holloway Prison.

Initially charged with conspiracy, her case was eventually tried under the archaic Witchcraft Act of 1735. The trial garnered significant public and legal attention, culminating in a guilty verdict on the witchcraft charge, but acquittal on others. Sentenced to nine months' imprisonment, Duncan's conviction was one of the last under the Witchcraft Act, leading to its eventual repeal in favor of the Fraudulent Mediums Act, influenced partly by her case.

After her release, Duncan promised to cease conducting séances, though she evidently did not adhere to this pledge, as she was arrested again in 1956 during a séance. She died later that year, with some spiritualists attributing her death to injuries sustained during the police raid. Her story remains a contentious chapter in the history of British mediumship.

Harrison Odjegba Okene

Waking up to use the bathroom is typically an annoyance, but on May 26, 2013, it became a life-saving act for 29-year-old Harrison Odjegba Okene. By an incredible turn of fate, leaving his bunk to go to the restroom saved him from a shipwreck, making him the sole survivor and the only person known to have survived nearly three days on the seafloor.

The Gulf of Guinea, located in the southeast Atlantic Ocean, is known for its petroleum-rich layers of sedimentary seabed, attracting numerous offshore oil drilling operations along the African coast. On that fateful day, about 20 miles off Escravos, Nigeria, three tugboats were assisting a Chevron oil tanker at Single Buoy Mooring #3 in turbulent waters. Early in the morning, just before 5 am, the tugboat Jascon-4 was overturned by a massive rogue wave.

Due to ongoing piracy in the area, security measures required the 12-man crew to lock themselves in their rooms while sleeping, which unfortunately delayed their escape when disaster struck. However, Harrison, the ship's cook, was already up and in his underwear, having left his room to use the bathroom. As the vessel capsized and water surged in, Harrison struggled to open the bathroom's metal door against the fierce water pressure. Unable to reach the emergency hatch, he witnessed three of his colleagues being swept away by the water. The force of the water then pushed him through a narrow corridor into another bathroom attached to an officer's cabin. Despite being dazed and injured, he miraculously survived by clinging to an overturned washbasin to keep his head above water.

The boat sank almost 100 feet, resting upside down on the seabed. Immediate rescue efforts were launched with nearby boats and a helicopter, and a diving team located the wreck and marked it with buoys. Although Harrison responded to their signals by banging back, the divers, unprepared for a deep dive, did not hear him and eventually left after a brief search, assuming no survivors.

After spending nearly a day in the bathroom, Harrison ventured out into pitch darkness and discovered another air pocket in the engineer's office. Now with sufficient air, his next challenge was the cold. Deep below the surface, where temperatures are significantly lower than the pleasant 81.9°F found on the surface in May, Harrison faced the risk of hypothermia. He managed to improvise a platform from a mattress and stripped wall paneling to stay partially out of the water, conserving body heat.

Alone, cold, and in complete darkness, Harrison's thoughts turned to his family and his faith. Amid the terrifying sounds of the creaking hull and the sea creatures feeding on his fallen crewmates, he prayed for deliverance. As time passed, the harsh conditions began to take a toll, stripping the skin from his tongue and exposing him to the smell of decay, believed to be his deceased colleagues.

The parent company of the Jascon-4, West African Ventures, had contracted a deep-sea salvage saturation diving team from the subsea services company DCN Global to recover the bodies of the lost crew members. The dive operation on the Lewek Toucan, which included six divers, deck crew, and technical staff, was anticipated to be challenging. The complexity was compounded by the vessel having sunk upside down into soft mud, causing poor visibility due to stirred-up silt, and the boat's doors being secured from the inside for safety.

Dive team two, led by supervisor Colby Werrett and consisting of divers Nico Van Heerden, Andre Erasmus, and Darryl Oosthuizen, spent over an hour breaking through external watertight doors to access the boat. Inside, they faced disorienting conditions with the ceiling underfoot and the floor overhead, navigating through murky water filled with floating debris.

As the divers methodically searched the vessel, retrieving four bodies, Nico squeezed through the main deck stairs into a narrow passageway. Here, he encountered Harrison Odjegba Okene, who had nearly lost hope after hearing and responding to noises he thought were from the rescue team. Harrison had seen a diver's light but was unable to catch his attention in time. However, in a miraculous turn, Nico reached out, touching what he thought was another body, only for Harrison to squeeze his hand in response, confirming he was alive.

This unexpected survival threw the team into action. Recreational divers usually don't stay below 100 feet for more than 20 minutes due to safety protocols, but Harrison had been under for nearly 60 hours in an air pocket compressed by the ocean's pressure. Calculations suggested the air had just enough oxygen for him to survive that duration. Additionally, Harrison had been reducing carbon dioxide buildup by agitating the water, increasing its surface area for CO_2 absorption, delaying the reach of lethal levels.

To assist Harrison, divers warmed him with hot water and provided an oxygen mask. Discussions ensued topside with medical and diving experts on managing his decompression sickness risks. Known as 'the bends,' this condition could cause severe health issues if Harrison ascended too quickly.

Harrison was prepped with a diving helmet and harness, showing remarkable composure throughout the rescue. He was transported to the surface in a diving bell and then moved to a decompression chamber to adjust to surface pressure over several days.

Of the 12 crew members on the Jascon-4, divers found one survivor and recovered 10 bodies, with the search for the last crew member halted due to dangerous conditions.

Harrison made a full recovery but decided to retire from sea-based roles, influenced by survivor's guilt and commitments made during his ordeal, vowing never to return to the sea. He took up a land-based cooking job and continues to manage post-traumatic stress, including nightmares of being underwater. His ordeal and miraculous survival marked a profound turning point in his life.

The Bloody Benders

In the 1870s, Osage Township in Kansas was a quiet, small settlement along the Great Osage Trail, an ancient Native American route through this part of the Midwest. Travelers could choose to stay at the Wayside Inn, a modest establishment operated by the Bender family. However, guests often received more than they expected. The history of Osage Township, like much of the American Midwest in the 19th century, was influenced by the displacement of its Native American inhabitants. Following the end of the American War in 1865, the U.S. government relocated the Native Americans from Lebek County, Kansas, to a new reservation in Oklahoma. The vacated land was then distributed to homesteaders.

In 1870, the area around what would be known as Osage Township was acquired by five families of spiritualists, inspired by the religious fervor of the Third Great Awakening in mid-19th century America. One of these families was led by John Bender Sr., who arrived with his son John Jr., his purported wife Elvira, and her daughter Kate. John Sr., around 60 years old, and Elvira, in her early 40s, were possibly siblings rather than spouses, as some locals speculated. John Jr. was 25, and Kate was 23.

The Benders, believed to have originated from Germany or the Low Countries, were an enigmatic family. John Sr. struggled with English, while Elvira, or "Ma" as she preferred, feigned difficulty with the language despite her evident proficiency. John Jr. and Kate were more articulate and often spoke for their parents. The Benders worked to establish a comfortable existence in Osage

Township, building a cabin and barn by the end of 1871 and cultivating a vegetable garden and orchard.

Their home was divided into a simple dwelling and a general store that doubled as an inn, which they named the Wayside Inn. Although basic and drab, it provided necessary shelter for travelers needing a place to stay overnight. The family was considered odd by their neighbors. John Jr. was known for his random laughter, and Kate, claiming to be a healer, boasted of her ability to communicate with the dead, holding séances and giving lectures on spiritualism. Her advocacy of free love enhanced her notoriety, and the inn became a popular stop for men traveling the Great Osage Trail.

John Sr.'s presence left a strong impression on visitors, often described as brutish and lacking civility. He and Elvira were reclusive, while Kate and John Jr. were more sociable and even attended the local Sunday school. Despite John Sr.'s unwelcoming demeanor, travelers continued to frequent the inn, only to discover that it offered more challenges than just its unappealing aesthetics.

In early summer 1871, the body of a man named Mr. Jones was found in Drum Creek near the Wayside Inn, with no clear suspect despite the close proximity of the creek's owner to the crime scene. A few months later, two more bodies were discovered on the prairie close to Osage Township, bearing similar fatal wounds—cut throats and blunt force trauma—matching the condition of Mr. Jones. By 1873, the trail had become notorious for dangers such as horse thieves and the disappearance of travelers had become so infamous that many began to avoid the area altogether.

Vigilance committees were formed, but they often wrongfully detained innocent men, accused of being behind the disappearances. Although these men were later released by authorities, some fled the county under continued suspicion. Investigators tried to connect the dots following the prairie body discoveries near Osage Township, eventually realizing that both victims had stayed at the Wayside Inn, suggesting a pattern to the killings.

Kate Bender, known as a healer and an attractive young woman, was frequently visited by male guests. At the inn, unsuspecting guests were seated next to a canvas wall separating the inn from the family's living quarters. While distracted by Kate, either John Bender Sr. or his son would strike the guest from behind the canvas with a heavy, blunt object, likely a sledgehammer. Kate or her mother would then ensure the victim was deceased, finishing them off if necessary. Wealthier guests, likely to have cash or horses, were prime targets for such attacks.

After the murders, bodies were disposed of through a trapdoor into a cellar, later moved to the prairie, Drum Creek, or buried in the Bender's orchard. Among the victims were Ben Brown from Howard County, carrying a substantial amount of money, and W.F. McCrotty, who arrived with valuable horses and never left. In December 1872, George Launcher visited with his infant daughter, carrying $1,900, planning to relocate to Iowa. Both were murdered and buried in the Bender's orchard, with the horrifying revelation that the young girl was buried alive. Johnny Boyle was another victim, likely targeted for his horse and saddle.

The murders persisted into 1873, by which time the Benders had killed at least a dozen travelers. However, one of these killings finally triggered an investigation that would end the grim hospitality offered at the Wayside Inn.

In the spring of 1873, Dr. William Henry York, a friend of George Launcher who had been murdered by the Benders along with his daughter in December prior, decided to travel to Kansas using the same route the Launchers had taken. Concerned about his friend's silence, Dr. York passed through Osage Township in mid–March 1873 but subsequently vanished. His disappearance triggered an extensive search led by his brothers, prominent figures in the Midwest. One of them, Colonel Alexander York, a Civil War veteran, lawyer, and Kansas State Senate member, arrived at the Wayside Inn on March 28,

1873. The Benders confirmed Dr. York had stayed with them but claimed he left the following day, possibly falling prey to trail hazards.

Colonel York considered this but remained suspicious, especially as local residents began sharing their misgivings about the Bender family. One woman recounted being chased by Mrs. Oliveira Bender with a knife. When Colonel York returned on April 3 to confront the Benders, Oliveira vehemently denied the accusations, branding her accuser a witch and unexpectedly revealing her proficiency in English—a fact she had previously concealed.

Despite Oliveira's protests, the colonel's companions were convinced of the Benders' guilt and pushed for an arrest and a property search. However, Colonel York demanded solid evidence first. Meanwhile, Kate Bender tried to lure the colonel back alone, promising to use her clairvoyance to locate his brother. During a public meeting at the local schoolhouse, attended by both Benders and 75 locals, it was decided to obtain a search warrant for every homestead between Big Hill Creek and Drum Creek, including the Benders'.

Days later, a local farmer noticed the Bender property was abandoned and alerted the authorities. A search party led by Colonel York discovered the property hastily vacated and found signs of foul play, including blood residue and fresh graves in the orchard. They unearthed a grisly scene—a makeshift graveyard with multiple victims, including Dr. York's brother.

Investigations revealed the Benders' true identities: John Flickinger, his son John Gebhardt, Almira McGriffis, and her daughter Eliza. The family had fled, their abandoned wagon found outside Thayer, 12 miles from the inn. They likely headed southwest by train, with the younger Benders possibly moving towards Texas or New Mexico, while John Sr. and Oliveira took a different route to Missouri. Despite large bounties, the trail soon went cold.

The Bloody Benders' fate remains a part of Western lore, with sporadic sightings and failed vigilante pursuits over the years. John Gebhardt vanished into West Texas, his whereabouts forever uncertain. There were rumors of the elder Bender's suicide in Lake Michigan in 1884 and a mysterious arrest in Montana, where a suspect fitting his description died trying to escape custody, making identification impossible.

In 1889, a mother and daughter arrested in Michigan for larceny were suspected of being Oliveira and Kate Bender. Despite some recognition from former acquaintances, the evidence was inconclusive, and they were released, allowing the Benders to evade justice for their 1870s crimes. Today, the Bloody Benders live on in American folklore, immortalized in books, TV shows, and films, their infamy enduring well into the 21st century.

Ilia Ivanov

Mythological creatures, from the elephant-headed god Ganesh in India to the jackal-headed god Anubis in Egypt, have always captured our imaginations. But what occurs when these ancient myths enter the realm of scientific pursuits? Human-animal hybrids not only epitomize the conflict between reason and primal impulses but also pose significant ethical dilemmas when brought into the real world.

Enter Ilia Ivanov, a Soviet scientist of the 1920s who sought to redefine the boundaries of established science by attempting to combine human and ape DNA. Contrary to popular belief, Stalin was not interested in creating a human-ape army. However, Ivanov did pursue his bold experiments during Stalin's rule, leveraging the government's anti-religious sentiment to obtain funding.

Ivanov's proposal was daring: he aimed to challenge divine supremacy by creating a new species, securing both funding and a journey to Africa. Despite his grand ambitions, he faced a major obstacle— the absence of human volunteers. His efforts to recruit local women in French Guinea faced staunch opposition. Persisting, Ivanov resorted to using sperm samples from his team to fertilize female chimpanzees. This approach also met challenges, and in desperation, Ivanov began to inseminate local women with chimpanzee sperm without their consent—an egregious breach of ethics that ultimately led to his downfall.

Back in Russia, Ivanov's problems compounded with scarce resources and increasing pressure. His vision was crumbling. In a final attempt, Ivanov sought volunteers, but only one distressed woman responded. Before any further experiments could occur, Ivanov was swept up in a political purge and exiled to Kazakhstan, marking the end of his controversial quest.

Ivanov's story is a poignant reminder of the crucial role of ethical standards in scientific research. The pursuit of knowledge should never override fundamental human rights and dignity. Although Ivanov's experiments ended, the quest for human-animal hybrids persists, raising profound ethical questions and sparking rigorous debates. Advancements in science now allow exploration into cross-species experiments, yet we must ask ourselves: just because we can, does it mean we should?

The controversy over human hybrid research has resulted in funding pauses, potentially delaying progress in fields such as stem cell research. Despite the moral reservations, some proponents argue that chimera research could yield valuable insights into human biology and lead to advancements in medical testing and organ transplantation, possibly reducing organ rejection rates.

The moral and ethical concerns surrounding the creation of human-monkey embryos are significant, yet the scientific potential remains compelling. While some nations have outright banned human hybrid research, others advocate a case-by-case evaluation, striving to balance knowledge advancement with ethical considerations. As we confront these burgeoning scientific capabilities, we must heed the lessons from Ilia Ivanov's story: with great power comes great responsibility, and our quest for knowledge should never compromise our humanity.

The Pepsi Navy

There's a persistent rumor circulating on the internet that at one point PepsiCo received several ships from the USSR, purportedly making it the owner of the sixth largest navy in the world at that time. This claim inevitably prompts the question: Did it actually happen? The story varies significantly, with some versions suggesting it occurred after World War II, others in the 1960s, and yet others in the 1980s. However, the transaction actually took place in 1989.

So, what exactly was this transaction? Pepsi wanted to continue selling its beverages in the large Soviet market, but faced a challenge: the Soviet ruble was a closed currency, essentially valueless outside the USSR, and could not be exchanged for dollars. This restriction meant foreign companies could not repatriate their profits. To address this, Pepsi struck a deal in the 1970s with a Soviet vodka company, allowing some vodka sale profits globally to compensate for Pepsi's Soviet sales.

However, as Pepsi began losing money, it renegotiated the terms. It was reported in the US that the USSR would pay for continued Pepsi sales with decommissioned naval vessels. These ships were to be sent to India and scrapped to reimburse Pepsi. Some media outlets claimed the deal included 17 submarines, a frigate, a destroyer, and a cruiser. Despite such reports, this fleet would not have ranked as the sixth largest navy globally, not even placing in the top 30, though it would have been impressive for a private company.

Yet, there's a twist: the actual transaction never involved naval warships. The idea of selling ships for scrap was proposed by the Soviet government but was never realized. Every ship in the Soviet navy accounted for during that period was not part of this deal. Instead, the USSR agreed to build cargo ships for Pepsi, which the company could sell or lease as needed.

Thus, despite the intriguing narrative, Pepsi never owned a navy. Even if it had, it wouldn't have been particularly large. Nonetheless, the deal, finalized in 1989, lasted 18 months before the USSR's collapse forced Pepsi to start negotiations anew.